cacophony
of bone

Also by Kerri ní Dochartaigh

Thin Places

cacophony of bone

of bone

the circle of a year

kerri ní dochartaigh

MILKWEED EDITIONS

For permission credits see p. 287

Published 2023 by Milkweed Editions
Printed in Canada
Cover illustration by Vasilisa Romanenko
Cover design based on work by Rafaela Romaya
Author photo by Manus Kenny
23 24 25 26 27   5 4 3 2 1
First US Edition

Library of Congress Cataloging-in-Publication Data

Names: Dochartaigh, Kerri ní, 1983- author.
Title: Cacophony of bone / Kerri ní Dochartaigh.
Description: First US edition. | Minneapolis, Minnesota : Milkweed Editions, 2023. | Summary: "Cacophony of Bone is an ode to a year, a place, and a love that changed a life; it is a book about home-the deepening of family, the connections that sustain us."-- Provided by publisher.
Identifiers: LCCN 2023013512 (print) | LCCN 2023013513 (ebook) | ISBN 9781571311573 (hardback) | ISBN 9781571317827 (ebook)
Subjects: LCSH: Dochartaigh, Kerri ní, 1983- | Authors, Irish--21st century--Biography. | Nature--Psychological aspects. | Home--Psychological aspects. | Ireland--Social life and customs--21st century. | LCGFT: Autobiographies.
Classification: LCC PR6104.O22 Z46 2023 (print) | LCC PR6104.O22 (ebook) | DDC 828/.9203 [B]--dc23/eng/20230726
LC record available at https://lccn.loc.gov/2023013512
LC ebook record available at https://lccn.loc.gov/2023013513

Milkweed Editions is committed to ecological stewardship. We strive to align our book production practices with this principle, and to reduce the impact of our operations in the environment. We are a member of the Green Press Initiative, a nonprofit coalition of publishers, manufacturers, and authors working to protect the world's endangered forests and conserve natural resources. *Cacophony of Bone* was printed on acid-free 100% postconsumer-waste paper by Friesens Corporation.

For my bábóg,
the light that came to stay.

But on this All Souls' Night there is
no respite from the keening of the wind.
I would not be amazed if every corpse came risen
from the graveyard to join in exaltation with the gale,
a cacophony of bone imploring sky for judgement
[. . .]
On a night like this I remember the child
who came with fifteen summers to her name,
and she lay down alone at my feet
without midwife or doctor or friend to hold her hand
and she pushed her secret out into the night
[. . .]
On a night like this I number the days to the solstice
and the turn back to the light.

Paula Meehan

The words you are about to read were written in a small stone cottage, a mere handful of kilometres away from the resting place of the stone narrator of the poem above; the statue of the Virgin at Granard.

The words you are about to read are in memory of the child of which the stone statue speaks, and of *her* child.

This book is in memory of Ann Lovett and her baby boy Patrick, who both died during his birth, on a bitter cold night, with only stone statues there by their sides, in the very heart of Ireland.

Prologue

I AM TELLING YOU HERE
OF a year
that was like
no other.

I AM TELLING YOU HERE
of a year
that was just the same
as every other that
had ever gone before.

Two days after winter solstice in 2019 I journeyed across an invisible border, from the North of Ireland to the South – to a small stone railway cottage – on a ghost line cutting through the heart of Ireland.

Moving – flitting from place to place like a migratory bird – is all I've known. I've averaged a house per year for each one I've spent on the earth, and then, suddenly – somehow – I found myself sowing seeds in the earth, painting a front door yellow – feathering a safe nest, for the very first time.

What does it mean to stay put?

The only full year I spent in that cottage, a handful of kilometres from the statue of the Virgin at Granard, the outside world changed shape and colour entirely.

We were asked not to leave the island of Ireland for the whole year.

For most of that year we were held within the same land-locked county.

For some of it we were locked down to within 2 kilometres of our single-roomed, isolated home.

But maybe the events of that year really started with finding the nests.

When I began to brood, not over a clutch but over *time*.

When I began to try to sculpt it, day by day, alone, wandering, again and again, without scale or horizon, the same field, the same lane, the same stretch of wet, hungry land. When I stepped, in a way, outside & inside, above & below – the flow of it all, the flow of my own blood; enough to really let those objects come. To notice those things and to hold them, give my furry body over to their coming, to stop hurrying through life like a person shamed, by my female body and its traumas, by my past, by what that body could not have, what its parts could not produce.

The objects, when they came, swept me with them in their flow, and rattled my bones.

> Creamy-white dove eggs, opened but unbroken;
> the skull of a badger, too sculpted to even seem real;
> on Mother's Day (my heart cracked open like a dry seed-
> head), a perfect, otherworldly antler, from the field's exact
> middle;
> I took, I took, I took.

Bone after bone, porcelain white and willowy: sheep and deer, horse and fox – the pelvic girdle of a delicately bird-like rat – objects so creaturely as to make the longing that had grown inside me slowly, quietly, ease.

There were birds, that year, so many of them as to seem unthinkable.

There was a wren, always a wren; that year was the year of the wren.

And you see, it really happened in this way, and I really can tell it to you no other way than this. At the bottom of that laneway, objects came from everywhere, ordinary and flawed, on days when time and place no longer knew the way, and I took them.

I took every single thing into my arms and hands and home, that year; I was compliant.

I knew at every turn I could not go back to how I lived before the objects came. They were an invitation I could do nothing but accept.

Time did the things it does when we aren't looking, and soon my lover began, while walking on his own, to find things too. Things, you understand, that never once had come his way before that year. His nests were, to my eye, more gorgeous than my own, but I felt no jealousy. It was such sweet relief to speak of those objects, of what I saw them as taking the place of, somehow. We sat, each night, as the names of those we'd lost were read aloud and we mourned for those we did not know, behind the daily count; faces we had not seen but could not turn away from now. A silence took up residence; it lay in circular objects, things we knew had once been crafted by the careful, repeated movements of the bodies of birds.

You lost, too.
You grieved.
You wondered when it all might end; if ever.

The grief, the one I went there first to bury, still came in waves, as we all have known it to; the deep water that none of us will ever fully swim through. It paled, though, so incredibly, in the face of the sorrow of those days. I held it to the sky and watched it fade. I saw its steely greys and charcoals water down. I watched the ache for what I did not have turn chalky, I stood and let the fledglings drink its milk. It sounds formulaic, as though I forced it in some way, but that year came to me like a field of bleached white bones.
I can't go back to who I was before that year.

That time was like no other, all of us thought – but we knew it was exactly like any other, too. The swallows arrived at my new home, found safe sanctuary, and built their nests.

They arrived with you, too, if they had in other summers,
just like before.
You stood and watched them fill the sky like a song.
You laughed.
You cried.
You noticed them.
You didn't.
The longest day came, as always it does – and the shortest
came, too – in turn.

   I am trying to tell you about time.

That oddly boned creature, how it shapeshifts, right before our
eyes. How we cannot stop or change it, how it slows down,
or moves so fast we cannot keep a hold of it; no matter how
we might long to, no matter how firm our grasp.

I am trying to tell *myself* about time, rather.

I found out I was pregnant in the second week of August 2020,
in the second season of a global pandemic, in the first summer
in my new home, as night fell in my first garden.

Everywhere was still and warm.
Moths fluttered above our heads,
pulled towards the lights
that had only just gone on
in our small quiet stone cottage.

Eanair, January

Old Moon

Wolf Moon

Cold Moon

Moon After Yule

Frost Moon

Ice Moon

Hard Moon

Great Moon

Severe Moon

Spirit Moon

Greetings Moon

Frost Exploding Moon

Canada Goose Moon

Moon of Frost in the Tepee

· Centre Moon

Before

It began two days
after the winter solstice,
as all stories begin:
with light.

It began with a flock of birds, signalling something, half-sentences scrawled by clawed feet, that we could not quite divine.

The light on that raw, post-cusp morning was unreliable; it shifted and spat, coughed and spluttered like an old hound by the side of a rusted shipping container. The person the light was waiting for did not come, and we lay in their place instead, beneath its grief, its phlegmy, sea-green bane.

In limp and ceaseless sleet, my lover drove our Transit, below a metallic dove-grey sky flecked with starlings. Those oily-feathered, maundering ghosts tailed us across an invisible border, from Derry in the north-west of Ireland to the bottom of an isolated, mucky laneway in the back end of nowhere. Particular creatures, like particular places, have evolved in ways conducive to the act of being read. Others remain knotted, thorny as the overgrown dreamscapes of childhood, their slanted scripts indecipherable.

Other creatures lingered, too,
in the backcloths of that
flitting, ashen, winter's day.

Ones for which I'd pined and longed, hoped and begged.

Those other creatures were, it must be told, not coming at all, in fact − and those creatures were the reason why we moved here, to this abandoned, stony railway line, in the musty heart of the winter. I came to grieve those unborn things, those creatures that I could not coax to land. That laneway seemed the place that I might mourn them, mark their echoey, empty absence, on a forgotten stretch of land. I came to change my life, which is, of course, the reason any of us go anywhere; we take to sea and sky and land so we might learn, once more, to breathe.

I would sculpt a fine, full life without a child.

I would loosen.
I would soften.
I would cry.
I would be quiet.
I would walk the fields.
I would get a dog.
I would write.

I would nourish, instead of creatures, words.

We have lived together, my lover and I, in three different houses before this one − all in the north of the island, in my hometown, the city of Derry. The internet tells me the average person will live in seven different houses in their lifetime. Before that winter in which our lives & bodies & days & belongings became as intertwined as ivy on an old sycamore, he had lived (if we have counted them all properly) in 23 houses and I in 34. We moved into this cottage two days after the winter solstice of 2019, a handful of weeks before the UK left the EU, another handful of weeks before the most life-altering collective experience many of us have ever known: the arrival of Covid 19 into our bodies & our nightmares, our consciousness & our world.

My partner inherited the cottage two summers before we moved into it. It felt so obvious to us that we would simply move there, to this house. That we would change almost everything in our lives beyond all recognition. We did not really plan for it at all, so to speak. We fell into this new life without any real sense of having even talked any of it through, of having given such vast upheaval even a second thought. It was only us two, you see – no matter how much or for how long I had longed for it to be otherwise – so we had only ourselves to think of. We walked away from all that we knew in the course of a single month. Packed up a rented home. Shut down a small business. Said farewell to the small group of people we felt close to. Somehow it felt like the most ordinary thing – and the wildest – all in one foul swoop.

We arrived at this house in weather the like of which I had never really experienced before that night. I could not give one solitary jot about what might be referred to as *bad weather*, rain, hail, wind, snow, etc., etc., etc. I am very comfortable with the elements. I grew up on the north-west coast of Ireland so was left with very little choice. I am, too, a child born of the winter. *I am taken by storms, and I always have been.* I am particularly drawn to winter storms. I am drawn to their light, you see.

> Among the most difficult memories,
> well beyond any geometry that can be drawn,
> we must recapture the quality of the light
> *Gaston Bachelard*

A recollection of space and time . . .

. . . I am sitting through an English GCSE lesson in a cold Portakabin in a school that, within a decade and a half, will be deemed inappropriate for housing bodies and minds.

I hear, for the first time, the opening line of *Jane Eyre*.

I imagine, with no real understanding of why, that the lines will stay with me always.

I know, or I think I know, just how much there is to be said of such a moment as is conveyed in those famous words.

A moment in time that begins with wild weather, weather that will not be tamed. Weather that stops you in your place and holds on to you for dear life.

And so it was with that storm that, two decades later, carried me, with my lover, across a border on a small island – north to south – to settle here in its very centre. Metallic clouds, lilac strips across a violent grey sky, a violet halo around the storm's winter moon. Even the birds knew the weather in question 'meant something', so much more than what it really *should* have meant, of course. The starlings were the most clued in. They wheeled in the sky, trailing us as we tried to outrun them. All of us tucking our secrets in – beneath oxters that got wetter by the minute.

That very first night in our new home I began to dream of weather.

That first night I began to dream of a golden bird being thrown around by a fierce-faced wind, hung with silver thread; from an unnervingly bright-white moon.

The dream was unlike any I had ever really had before. It was nothing whatsoever like the dreams I've had since I started, and then stopped, drinking. My dreams have turned pedestrian, all the enchantment painted over with thick white paint. The light in that first night's dream was not really light at all in fact. It was more like a murmuration. The light was a gathering of pearlescent birds, sharing something with me that I couldn't quite interpret; beneath a brilliantly radiant, salmon-pink sky.

> *That first night*
> *I began to dream*
> *of a different*
> *kind of light.*

A kind of light I knew, early on, I would never be able to walk away from. I began to dream of a light that belonged to someone: someone I had not yet met. Light they would carry with them, from the very first moments when they arrived.

> (I am haunted by the light of things
> that I have not yet even known.

There is no metaphor
at play here.)

> Only bullshit.
> Only my own bullshit,
> that I cannot let go of for reasons
> such as melancholy, or laziness,
> or falseness, or fear.

I have forgotten the layout of almost every home I have lived in.
Where the kitchen was. If the doors opened in or out.
If there was carpet or wood beneath my feet.
If the garden had a wall, or a fence, or a gate:
even if there even was a garden at all.

But I could describe for you in minute detail the following things . . .
   The way the light fell in every room of every home I have ever lived in,
            in every season

                  at every time of day.

The light in almost every film I have ever watched, and in every storybook I have ever read.

How it danced & sang & called to me.

The light I grew up with

            and then ran from

                  over & over & over.

Light from days of loss; from days of love; from days of both.

The light when the swallows

            arrived & then

                  the light when they had to leave.

The light in the Bogside on the winter's evening I fell in love with my lover.
   Light that threw itself down in sleety slants on his overcoat as he walked away.
   The way it made an old black & white movie of the dreich Derry November night.
   The light on the first morning many years later when we woke up in our white Transit van outside our current home.

How it was like all the light in all the world had made its way here to this very laneway.

How it was like nothing I could really have believed was true before.

How it took me the whole day to realise it was the autumn equinox, and how that shocked me to my core; in a way akin to waking up in a stranger's bed.

Light has been my only constant.
Light has been my guiding star.

Snow light.
Storm light.
Northern light.

Southern light.
Home light
Hope light

I cannot get away from it, you see.
I cannot get away from light.

1st

I can never get my head around the fact they call this single day a new year, even though every day is a new day, a new beginning, a new everything. We want to tell ourselves that that particular day – the first one of the first month – is special in a way unlike all the others. We want to fool ourselves into believing in the linearity of existence, and in its order; even though every single thing is in flux; is ever turning & wheeling & piercing the sky, starling-like. Even though every single day feels like something I need to learn to mark, somehow . . . something I should embrace as though my life depended on it (because I think perhaps it does).

feathery sky
light like a river song
berries holding the water in prayer

Thrushes & wrens, crows & blackbirds.
Movement in the reeds that we cannot quite place.

A train – far off – carried in over the bog; displaces the silence. The dog & I, alone, in the same fields together for a week now. We never quite trace the same pathway. She never wants to leave the bottom stream, its pile of fallen branches, a winter pyre of ghost-bark; lichen-limb. I never want to leave the middle point. Imagining it as some form of thin place (though I beg myself to be done with all of that). Holding it as a portal, a threshold.

Have realised this is the first New Year's Day I didn't cry. Did not even come close.

What a fucking gorgeous thing, to walk into the year ahead feeling OK. Capable, even.

Shared John Kelly's 'Winter's Blessing' on Instagram, his 'un-expected birdsong / in the brief sun / of Sundays after Christmas'. P messaged: 'It did read "in the grief sun" and it would have been right as well' and I told her I needed to write that down somewhere. I didn't tell her, this bright winter's day, that I need to keep her words close, to tuck them in under my oxters like I imagine I would a baby if there had ever been one – to tuck them in beneath my skin like a charm. Words seem to grow so much more meaningful these days. Not in how they sound, or how they read, more in how they ring out in the middle of the night. When worry wraps around the door like those draft snakes, sleep refusing to come, no matter how calmly I call it.

2nd

3 years have gone by already but still I see that sliver of a crescent moon that arrived just as she died.
Florence.
Granny Flo.
The most curious, many-sided, wild woman ever I have known.
(No, I did not know you; no one could.)

3rd

Back in the fields after a day away (too long by far).

> Ghost limbs. Sleeping sky.
> Bleakest of beauties.

4th

A single candle in the window.
Never quite sure who, exactly, it is that I am trying to lead back home.
It is someone, though, that much I know.

5th
The dog is just so full of joy. It is contagious.

6th
After the hail, a soft, still light.
First visit to Castlepollard Library, just around the corner from the Mother and Baby Home.
I have so many thoughts on this but somehow cannot find a way to bring them up and out.
Swan children – all green and sculpted – beneath a swan moon in the square.
What do we do to undo it all, if even we can?
Starlings, so many of them, crying for everything worth crying for.
Nollaig na mBan evening spent grinding coffee and reading old Devonian dialect for Word Hoard Project in spring. So much to look forward to, I must remind myself.

7th
Storm field.
The dog and I both struggled to leave a particular tree, in the bone field, right beside the stream that borders the space. I am unsure why. It felt, surreal as this sounds, like a form of communion.
Swim in freezing Lough Derravaragh (more an immersion than a swim, perhaps).
More Children of Lir, of course. Coots calling, swans swimming, grey lifting.
Drive, in driving rain, past the railway line in the central bog of Ireland.
All rust, and things that are in the process of coming to an end.
Found it profoundly moving, for many reasons, I think.
Then, to bed with *Orison for a Curlew*. These words by Horatio

Clare feel almost too much to even process: 'The unknowable
has a pristine beauty and a wonder with no end.'
On a night as storm-bright as this one, there still is hope. There
still is beauty. There still is wonder with no end.

8th
Blue sky.
I can feel the turning.
Lichen-limbs, like a lament for the light.
World-womb, fallen branches in the middle field, ready to be
burned.

9th
Bought, for the small yellow Formica table, two wooden chairs
for a fiver.
I suppose this means we have a kitchen now.
Giving thought to what it means to listen.
All I thought I knew was nothing, nothing at all, in fact.
Earth, unteach me the world's ways. I want to learn yours.
How to write the grief that we all are carrying.
How not to hollow ourselves into a pit of fear, of worry, of
helplessness.
How to act, despite it all.

10th
Things, so many of them, touched by frost.

A line that halved and divided,
That ran alongside the trauma and the ache
– deep inside the bones of us
– the bones of the place;
What to do with all the bones,
As white as old man's beard
– on the circle of this darkling winter?

> (make a moon of them,
> make a moon of them)
> MAKE A MOON FROM THESE
> BROKEN, BRILLIANT BONES
> (you will always know the way /
> you will always know the way /
> YOU WILL ALWAYS KNOW.)

11th

When was the last time you wept?
When was the last time you laughed?

12th

S wrote, for CAAKE, about the importance of safe spaces. I howled at a moon I could not see, so moved by it all; how a man could be so tender, so honest, so good.
Another storm.

13th

First new moon after winter solstice.
Not long ago, people went into the woods, cut a branch of an oak and carried it in procession, into the folds of the sacred grove. Branches were consecrated for them to carry into their homes, in turn. There is a part of me that grieves the loss of such ceremony, such work for idle hands.
The moon is in labour tonight, bleeding out the old her, birthing the new. Nothing is linear with time, of course. Nothing ever ends. Every single object steps in & out of the circle of darkness that holds up the light. Light that drips and sings.

Reading, always as if for the first time, Annie Dillard. Have written this out and taped to the wall above my desk for when I feel so alone I cannot imagine ever crawling back up: 'These are our few live seasons. Let us live them as purely as we can, in the present . . . Living is moving; time is a live creek bearing changing lights . . . I like these slants of light; I'm a collector.'

14th

Found, as the last light slipped away, a field full of bones.

15th

Spent the whole day in bed with grief.
It never goes away, we only learn new ways to try to live alongside it.
Returned, before dark fell, to the horse carcasses in the field.
Thought, once more, as often I do, of Doireann Ní Ghríofa's words.

18th

A world touched and breathed upon by ice and frost.
The River Inny, loud and fierce, as the sun set on a pink and quiet world.
The first snowdrops.

19th

A halved white moon.
An image on Instagram, by an artist called Shelley Jackson, of snow with the word MOVING spelled out. Deeply, unimaginably *moving*, is the only word for it. I know that to keep moving is my only hope at getting through this time, this fog. I have started swimming in loughs as a way of embedding myself in the place and its past. I am ridiculous, and I know it, is the thing. I tell myself that I will stop being the kind of person who places such importance on things that really matter not a jot. Who gives a hoot how I spend my mornings. How cold the water. How salty the tears?
To walk is to know that you are in place.

To swim is to know that you are not in place.
That you never could be.
To swim is to know that you are liquid, ever changing, always flowing.
Moving. Always moving.

(The moths that seemed to have eased have, in fact, upped their numbers in ways to be almost surreal.)
White, of course.
Aways outside the field window, and always white.

20th
Ghost-winged dusk.
Purple all day and night and all of the parts in between.

21st
Storm light again.
Bog oak turned up and over in the lower field.
What might it feel like to be buried deep in the soil, then spat out to the surface?
To be returned?

22nd
Sonsie.
Drawing of the horse skull from days back – accompanied by this word.
Unsure, now, where I found it, or even what it means. Trying to learn this language, the one of my blood & bones, feels like trying to pull a tooth by candlelight in a storm.
(*I'm here for it*, though, as they like to say.)

Swimming where the sky and the water are as one.
Lines & land.
Where the cold and my bones learn to dance.

Stillness & swans & surrender.
Fog-breath, ice-lung lough.
Mist & mackerel in the sky.
The meeting of moments.
Birds & belonging.
Blurred life & lines.

23rd
The world has been hidden away from all view.
A snipe calls but I do not see it, of course.

Floored by Anne Enright's *No Authority*.
What a thing it is to be female on this island, on this earth.
Later, in the fog, on the laneway – firecrests.

24th
Foggy, freezing swim in the lough this morning.
Then, into the fields, as a skein of geese flew overhead.

Lough Derravaragh
Icy cold lough, swimming beneath a howling, grey sky as swans
held fast to the surface. Thoughts of children and voices, of
singing and bells, of wandering and exile. Wondering what it
might mean to belong somewhere. What it might mean to stay.
I have never before been held by water as cold as this.
I have never before been held by land as gentle and as silent.

Lough Owel
Swimming where the sky and the water meet, in a fog-breath,
ice-lung lough.
   Stillness and swans and surrender. Silence and stones and
searching. Thoughts on the way the heart holds room for oh
so much, for more than one vessel can contain, more than one
lifetime could ever fully know.
   (I am listening and I am looking, with everything that I have.)

25th
Artists' talk in Derry. We explored, with participants, the line that runs along the River Foyle.
Self, loss, finding, making, healing, making, circling, walking, creating, connecting and being.
Had not, by any reckoning, been prepared for the grief I would experience returning there, to both the place and all that is tied up with it.

26th
The ghosts of us, the lay of the land.
Back to the bone field, and all it holds for my insides.

27th
Editorial call for *Thin Places* (TP). Topic of motherhood came up, which I somehow had not expected, although I wonder how I could so readily ignore the obvious, even this many drafts in. Why am I so scared to explore this part of the past? For this is also my present. What do these segments of time – the then and now – mean for my future, my relationship with M, with myself? What do I need to do to finally make peace with it all? (I am so, so done with this grief.)

28th
Sneachta.

29th
An Irish newt, where the two lower fields meet (or separate) and I am so shook by it.
Some days the loneliness is fiercer than others and I can't work out the formula.
(Thoughts on wild, seemingly silent places, on grey and amber skies, etc., etc., etc.)
Grateful for Sara Baume's words in exquisite new book *Handiwork*: 'I believe it does not matter at all; I believe it is all that matters.'

30th
Terrifyingly icy swim.
Lough Léinn, oh my.
Notes on the silence of winter (or its unreality).
On how much, how deeply, we need this (almost) silence.

31st
Blue candle beside the yellow daffodils from yesterday.
My heart is breaking for the UK.
Brigid's Eve.
Red cloth is out.
Googled the making of the cross but don't have it in me to try today.
Reading all day about Ann Lovett and her baby and I am broken by it.
By what this country has done (continues to do) to its women and its children.

Tomorrow – the second month.
Have been thinking so much about the calendar; time in relation to space.
The widely accepted premise that we can make a standard, 'normal' perception of reality, of our lived experience.
How time is given meaning through narrative.
How stories fill in the gaps between time and place.
How I am unsure if I will ever be able to live, to flow, in this way.

the light the light the light

A friend talks to me of a church called the Church of Storms and I become incomparably obsessed with it. I want nothing more than to go there; to lay down on its cold floor – carved, curved beams above me – and sleep. I stand at the sycamore tree in the big field, the only place I can get 3G, and read everything I can about it. Built in the twelfth century on a beach, most likely the only church on a beach in all of Cornwall. Nestled beneath a rocky outcrop, within spitting distance of where the wild Atlantic meets the land. I read that it is held as a 'small pilgrim place'. Somewhere where all people of goodwill might pause on their journey. I don't want to think of the church, somewhere I have only seen on the screen of my phone, in this way. I do not wish to see this storm church as being one of many designated stops on a route through an island. I don't want to be able to hover above a virtual map and find my nearest stop, a place fulfilling its purpose, for the website, 'of making space, keeping silence, encouraging solitude, and providing simple focus'. I want the church only as a storm church. I want things that are ridiculous, nonsensical, selfish.

I want to stop time.

I   want   to   undo,   redo   and ᐧ then   undo again.

I want to lay down, alone, in the storm church, and wait until it all feels OK.

(Will it ever feel OK?)

I find myself searching for the words of others as means to fill the holes that the actions of (other) others have left in me. Some words take up more space than others, of course. When I first began sending my work out to try to find a place for it, a home for my own words, a writer I deeply admire offered me the most incredible advice I could ever have hoped for. I wrote their words out and taped them onto the front of my laptop because I didn't have a designated space at which to write, no desk to stick them above, no room of my own in which to read them to myself out loud. I still don't have any of these things (this is only somewhat true, in fact). My lover has started to build me, in the corner of our small single-roomed living space, a desk at which to write. So now I *do* have, in actual fact, a fraction of these things. I will tape their words to the wee bit of wall above me when it is ready.

I offer their words to you, too. A gift passed from one to the other like a giggling babe: REMEMBER THE LIGHT.

To give a little context, I was writing about the darkest experiences of my entire life, in the work they were reading the earliest drafts of. We had, this writer and I, encountered one another only through Instagram. Even still, many years and correspondence later, we have yet to meet in real life. The only sense of one another that we had back then was what we observed through a small handheld rectangle. Since that time we have spoken on FaceTime, on the phone, on Zoom, but in those early days our relationship consisted solely of images – handpicked but unfiltered on both our parts – shared with our respective followers. It would be at least a year after the LIGHT feedback before we began to send one another images through Instagram messaging; private images that no one else was privy to. They liked lots of my images, if not all of them. I did the exact same in return. Upon rereading this sentence it sounds as though this clicking of the heart-shaped button was transactional in some way, as though we were merely purchasing Christmas presents for the other's child in return for a gift sent to our child (neither of us were parents back then), but really it was not this way at all. We simply, without ever having met, were fired by lots of the same things. We had many shared (but separate) experiences. There was lots of crossover between our individual past lives; lots of the things that made us who we were seemed as closely aligned as to create a mirror. When I looked at their images, coupled with the words chosen to sit alongside, it often felt as though this person and I should meet (and they often said this, too). The thing is that recently I have begun to wonder if perhaps we did meet, this writer of the light, just once – many moons ago. There is a photo of this writer from quite some time ago, long before the light message, back when we both had a strong connection with the same city. In the photo they are wearing a pin on their coat, one I recall someone who looked exactly like them wearing, in a small vintage shop in the old town of the city in which I lived for the ending of my twenties. I am not trying, in any way, to hide away the identity of the writer here, the one who has now become a friend. There is no need for me to keep anything about them from you. In fact a number of readers will likely be able – even with just the information afforded here – to work out exactly who I am speaking of. The thing is, though, back then, back when this person offered me those words – the thing that was most significant of all was the fact that despite our use of the like button and all our lovely comments on each other's posts, despite the fact we both loved so many of the same things and had many shared experiences, we were complete and utter strangers. Even if we did meet in that small vintage shop that no longer exists, all we may have said to one another was 'Hello' – in that way that people have of greeting one another that says that they do not wish to talk, really, but that they know it really is important, in the very least, to acknowledge – in a space as small as to be almost claustrophobic – the existence of the other. If it *was* them, the thing I recall, aside from the pin and their beautiful hair, was heavy rain falling on cobblestones, so that it made a film of the grey, passing moment, somehow.

Anyway, back to *the light*.

What does it mean to consider light?

What happens when we notice it, observe it, mark it, meditate upon it?

What does it mean to honour light?

What might we mean when we say we are drawn to it?

That perhaps it is the only thing that makes some days feel manageable, real, safe?

What might it mean to live those days as an ode to light, no matter how fucked up the world were to become?

(What does it mean to remember light?)

Back to the light.

Back to remembering it.

Back to, rather, remembering being told to remember it.

What did this person mean by these words, which are nothing other than a gift?

(When I first typed the sentence above, by some trickery, some magic, the sentence came out as it is typed below. I toyed, for quite some time, with the idea of leaving it that way.)

What did this person mean by these words, which are *nothing offer than a gift?*

And now:

allow me

to offer them

to you,

the gift of those words.

REMEMBER THE LIGHT.

Feabhra, February

Snow Moon
Storm Moon
Hunger Moon
Bear Moon
Eagle Moon
Moon of the Dark Red Calves
Bony Moon
Chaste Moon

Why the moths came . . .

And do you know, even now,
in the thick of it, as they
blend into this place like
the gloaming
becomes night,
as they land on my skin
like whitethorn
on the soil;
even now, still,
I could not tell you
why they came.

I had been making ready to leave, as I always seem to be, as I
always thought was the way that everyone experienced place.

It Was Winter

The land was being visited each day by a light that was metallic, shifting. There seemed to be a silence to my evenings I had never before encountered, and I wondered if it was this newly born, curious hush – in Derry, a city that in reality had started once more to violently, deafeningly riot – that was making me dream of snow.

I was getting everything in order in the only way I had ever known how. I was undoing all the threads that tied me to that oak-bounded, ghost-bordered city: boxing up books to offer a bookselling friend, donating dried goods, giving away most of what I owned, loosening the ties – in any way that felt fitting – to people, and experiences, objects and memories, held within its haunting, ancient walls. Cutting, breaking, clearing. I was shedding. I was making ready to leave the city in which I was born, one in which unfathomable trauma had winged its way into my life, like the night birds of some echoey and unending keen. I counted them up one night, watching the fire's embers die a slow death, those places I had left behind. It was the week before the winter solstice – the part of the year where the circle and the line meet – and a helicopter in the northern sky was making shadows on the terraced street. In a fortnight's time I would be turning thirty-six, averaging almost a house per year, for each and every one on this turning, burning earth.

Time has done the funniest of things since they came along. Not the stuff of speeding up and slowing down, neither the stuff of stopping – the only way I can put this is to say that time has become erratic, hard to catch – to hold – identify. You think it's there and that you are moving along with it, and that it is passing, unfurling, opening, marching, trickling, flowing, and everything. But then you realise it isn't. It just, and simply, *is not*. It is not moving. It is not carrying you anywhere. It is flighty. It is sometimes shimmering, at others it is see-through. Time has become light-like and winged; shall we say *lighty*? (I wish I knew the right words, but I will keep trying.) I want to make it as clear for you as my limited understanding can seek to make it.

Time shifted when they came but also it didn't at all, not even nearly. It changed colour and shape but these things aren't really the thing, you see. Really it was only ever these two things in the first place: flighty, lighty; a place, you might imagine, that goes and that comes, and sometimes we enter, and sometimes we stand and watch it from afar. And sometimes that ebb and flow grows legs and antennae – wings and feelers – shell and pincers, and sometimes we draw near but most of all we cannot reach it, we cannot touch it. It is gone. All I need to try to get down here with you is the fact that time showed itself that winter, dancing far outside my grasp, as well as being right there – in the mud beneath my feet, in the dirty bathroom, at traffic lights, on buses, in food, on and between book pages, in dreams, sent from ex-lovers, wrapped in the cloths of the dead, on social media (on every media), in manuscripts, in my hair, on both my arms (but only my left hand, only on my right thigh). Time revealed itself that winter and it was fragile and darting, folkloric and murky. It was winter, have I told you that the winter had arrived?

Time was – for the whole of that winter, and throughout all its aftermath – a flickering thing, a glinting thing (a lost and then found and then repeat again thing), a sheening thing, a fiercely and questionably ethereal thing.

I suppose all I needed to say was that time, that winter, was an insect.

I arrived in this new home last year, you recall, just as night fell, just as the last week of December began. It goes without saying that I arrived to find them already there, on that flitting, winter's night, in a house I barely even knew. They had come, it seemed, in an uncountable, unbidden number. They waited at the front door, long fallen out of use – boarded up for over a decade against the outside world and all that it contained. The markings on their wings were varied, memorable, exquisite. It will not, I suppose, surprise you when I tell you that they followed me inside. That they made themselves at home in this stone railway cottage, sought out corners and cobwebs, nooks and crannies. They made room for themselves in parts of that small dwelling I had not before known were there.

It is an uncomfortable detail, you will understand, but I failed to ask the moths to leave, that night.

I began, slowly, as I know you know, to write of them.

I drew their forms with pencil marks at dawn . . .

. . . 'It was winter . . .'

After being alone for a long time, one starts to listen
differently,
to perceive the organic and the unexpected all around,
to brush against all the incomprehensible beauty of the material.

Tove Jansson, 'The Island'

I have spent a lifetime navigating immeasurable layers of loneliness.

To try to write of those layers – each so different from the
other as to seem like bone & feather, each so similar as to seem
like bone & feather – feels ridiculous, pathetic, pointless.

The layers began to place themselves down on top of one
another very early on. I watched them pile up like damp coats
in front of a coal fire, like washes of colour on a wet page,
like bodies in a heartbreakingly achy scene.

The middle of my life thus far felt the loneliest of all. Until
the other parts of my life arrived in turn. Once, back then,
when I was a very different version of the person I am now,
I vowed to spend my life alone. I was a teenager, and full of
bulging, pulsating, hideous grief. Grief I had no idea what to
do with, that came out of nowhere and left me baying and
bawling; that rattled me like an easterly wind. Grief that only
ever seemed to shift when I touched myself until I saw extra
colours in place of lost shapes. I felt, back then, lonely no
matter who or what or when or where or why. I felt lonely
and I hated it. I felt lonely but when others were around I
wanted nothing more than to retreat; to go anywhere at all
where I could be lonely and actually be alone. Is this what it
means to be a teenager? Is this what it means to be a woman?
Is this what it means to be alive?

I have tried, at various points of my life, to write about these forms of loneliness, the differing types of solitude.

I see myself always as failing, always as having failed at this. I am unsure why it is that still I keep on trying.

I return, in life and in my days – over and over – to the poem 'Various Portents' by Alice Oswald. To her exquisite list of signs & warnings, exceptional & wonderful beings & things – and always I am taken by the desire to do the same for solitude.

I want to read about various solitudes, each more tender & raw, more beautiful & haunting than the one that came before. None as meaningful, as moving, as melancholic as the one that will follow. I know I cannot do this and make it sing, make it real, make it work – but I cannot shake this desire off me. I cannot put this loneliness to bed, cannot leave the various solitudes at the door and come inside to the warmth & companionship, the heat & the beat of others, their light.

And so, in moving to Correaly, another layer of loneliness found its way to the pile.

(What does it mean to leave room for such loneliness in spite of ourselves?)

It howled and raged and pelted, with the winds and sleet and rain, for two months straight, every weekend a new name given to the same weather, in the same season, until even the field became too treacherous to traverse. We took, us three, to keeping by the stove, tracking time not by the light, for there was none, you see, but by our animal needs: eating, drinking, emptying, warming, sleeping, mating (or not). January gave into the bowels of the winter. February slithered around my feet like an eel. There was, that year, an extra day to winter's count, a delicate, quite unreal gathering of hours, like small, clumped cells, and when it came it carried frost that reflected the light, a light too graceful to even try to capture, on film or paper – on screen or memory – it felt like winter was loosening its jealous, devastating hold. That day, the dog and I explored, a little, the milking barn beside our home, and I sat on a broken trailer, below the first blue sky of the year. It was the only thing that I really could call my own, and I wept. I cried for reasons I felt no need to take apart, for reasons I likely know but just as likely know I need not name. I cried until the dog dragged me, with her wildness, towards the outhouse. Its roof had long caved in, all traces of its purpose had been swept or flooded away, but still a sense of value, of purpose, filtered, like light, through rotted slats. Three objects found me there, in that ivy-clad, ghost-ruined space, only two of which I lifted from their hiding and brought, without a thought, into my home. I carried those objects – fallen, abandoned, beautiful – away from the damp corner of the shed, one smaller than the other but no less fine, as gently as I could, the most exquisite pair of nests.

1st

(On remembering light, still (and always).)

Imbolc.

Lá Fhéile Bríde, St Brigid's Day.

Stepping-stone between the seasons.

A bridge leading the way from winter to spring.

Started it with a muddy dog and words from Moya Cannon.

We drove, in the grey and fading light, to Athlone. Walked along the river, watching swans go about their daily work, listening to the groan and creak of the branches in the big winds. I am not really sure, most days, what it is that I should be doing. Feel unanchored, lonely, lost, but the light today, albeit short and seeming so far off, spurs me on. Can't shake the sense that there is something yet to come that holds an answer for me, or that holds the questions that I should, in fact, be asking.

On with the work, till then.

On with the words.

2nd

Candlemas

Light

Lanterns

Soil

There is a love that does not need words. I am nurturing it. I am trying to answer back. I am drawing the lines on my insides, silver winter tributaries on my bones.

(I am shook with the thought of how lonely I feel, shook by my own insides, and all that I can never fucking say.)

Read an excerpt from TP at the Imbolc festival in Derry.

Feels surreal to have crossed the border, to be back in the place I have only just left.
I wonder when this place will loosen its tight grip on me, release from its hold, cut me even just a little bit of slack.

3rd
First seaswim of the year, in Shroove, with R. Had not realised how much I needed the sea and female company. The dog's first time on the beach since she came to live with us, maybe first time ever – knowing a little of her early life. She was in her element. Creaturely joy is contagious.

4th
Home.
What a thing, to feel such relief on returning somewhere.
Was not expecting it to be honest.

5th
A more than half moon in the sky above the horses. I spend the day thinking of ways to connect that are not in person but that might feel more tangible, more meaningful, than online dialogue. I need to find ways to feel less alone here. Very glad to have M by my side but I know I need, for myself and for my work, to be around others too, in whichever shape that takes.

6th
Frost everywhere.
A muted, delicate pink sky filled with hundreds upon hundreds of crows.
I feel lonelier than I could ever have imagined feeling before now.
The hawk has been at work.
Feathers in the middle field, all that remains of a once winged thing.

7th

The storm is on her way. Saw, for the first time so far, waves on the lake.

An icy cold swim, in hungry winds, over limestone pebbles.

Arrived home to a package from R – two red candles and a pair of swimming gloves.

I wept, of course, for quite some time.

Walked in the field as the sun set with the most pounding headache. The colours of this incoming storm are divine, purples and greys with peachy orange strips, pale yellows cutting through; shards of stolen light.

I imagine writing a book only about storms.

Heading off in a small coracle in search of their beginning.

I sleep and dream of grey birds; ones that may or not be real; that I may or not have ever seen before.

8th

Before the bog rain, an excellent, sky-blue sky. (As if there could ever be simply one colour to the sky. How ridiculous.) Rereading *Bloodroot* by Annemarie Ní Churreáin. ('This hill . . . will answer in bog-tongue.') Every single time I am with her words I cannot help but weep at the beauty and the pain in equal measure. The older I get, the less able I am to stop the tears. I wish I could talk about that more, at all, even, but I let myself down again and again.

9th

Flooded fields, fallen boughs.

Storm-light, moon-flint.

('The sky was full of winter stars')

Reading, for the first time, Joseph Brodsky's *Watermark*, and making a promise to myself to return to both – to Venice, and to his words on Venice.

Scarlet elf cup on the trees by the stream, in the lower of the fields.

The Woodland Trust site tells me it has other names, too – red cap, moss cups, fairies' baths – and that in European folklore wood elves drank morning dew from the cups of this uncommon fungus.

I am suddenly overcome with the desire to share this with a small being, one that is mine (as if a person could *ever* belong to another in any shape or form); even one that brought them into the world.

Took it in my hands and held it, my hand resting on soft moss, red on green.

I am being reshaped by these fields and I am unsure yet if I am willing.

10th

L tagged me in a post on Instagram that made me weep and weep and weep. Two images of the moon – one I took, one she did – at more or less the same time yesterday.

The caption said: 'Same moon, 88 miles apart (as the crow flies) 'At 7.33 am this morning she was in full Leo. February's full moon is also known as the Snow Moon . . .'

She quoted, then, from another account: 'What are you ready to share? To speak into being? . . . Can you allow whatever has been on your heart to come forward?'

Well, can I?

I have no idea if I can, or how I would even begin.

Then, her own words at the end, just for me, I think: 'May it be so.'

Spent two hours under the yew tree in the field behind the house.
Wrote one word: Guardian.

Found, in the bone field, a shard of blue and white crockery, which made me instantly think of Doireann Ní Ghríofa, so I told her. Reading *A Girl's Story* by Annie Ernaux. Why should any other person try to write about life when writers like her already exist?
Just before the sun set this evening, I only just managed to save the dog from choking herself on barbed wire, waist high, in a black bog pool. She is the making and the breaking of me, I am convinced of it.

11th
Awoke to snow. Complete and utter joy without bounds.
Light that was all lemon and clouds so smoky grey as to make you want to lie down beneath them and wait for them to do their do in the morning's soft, breathy beginning.

12th
Parcel arrived from K including a book by a writer I have not yet encountered, Terry Tempest Williams – *When Women Were Birds*. Devoured it in one sitting. Dreamy and soothing and a call to action. Also inside was a hagstone on hemp to wear around my neck. When you are used to being hurt by women close to you, it is a feeling that cannot be put into words to experience such goodness from women you have not even met. I am humbled and more grateful than I know how to communicate, which saddens me, somehow.

13th
Galway in the light that belongs to the final breaths of winter, so we try to convince ourselves. I am ready for this one to be over; it has wounded me in funny old ways, as well as making my skin a little tougher. The way the light fell on the reeds seemed almost too gorgeous to be real.

14th
We marked today with seven candles lit, a rainbow of our own choosing. Like how we make a love of our own choosing (we try to, anyhow, which is the thing).

15th
Reading about gardening.
Am I really going to sow seeds into the earth?
Am I ready for that?

17th
Sat by stove after a fine day's work – a storm easing outside – beneath a sky-bright night.
I can see the end, just over a verge on the horizon; the third draft of TP is in its final stages. The dog is by my side. The radio is on. M is cooking. Candles are lit.
I am clean, I am warm, I am grateful.
Yesterday, Sunday, in by Correaly House, I was suddenly overcome by it: by gratitude. Watching small birds lift from the branches of the yew tree, into the arms of the storm. Thought of how many times I have felt so different from now. Dangerously so. How I could never imagine such a morning as yesterday.
Walked, today, in the bone field. Watched, over the fields and over the trees, for the very first time here, a heron. Hadn't realised how sorely I have missed them. Lots of work on the book, a lovely brunch of scone and egg, another stormy walk

with the hound. A rainbow, and so many tits in the cold air. Then, an exquisite sunset. Now, to read, finish letters and maybe write a little more. Beginning to feel a little overcome with the trawling back; the over & over & over again of things I would rather bury than excavate but today I feel strong and able for it all. (Wish to fuck it was always this way.)

The dog is asleep in her nest and I am so glad of her company in this place. So grateful for our life, us three.

Enjoyed, so much, Doireann Ní Ghríofa's new book; such a gift to us all.

The musician Andrew Weatherall died suddenly today, younger than M. Sad, and so many people seem badly affected. Death is such an odd thing. Such a vital part of this life yet we are, none of us, really quite equipped for it, I think.

M has lit the candle for dinner, and I love to watch these quiet, simple gestures that make up our days. Our lives are built of such small, quiet moments as those. Kettles boiled, candles lit, hands stroked, thanks given, bodies held in close as the day gives itself into the arms of dark night. Once I finish this draft I wonder how much more work there will be before I can say: done, finished, circle complete. And I wonder what there will be to do then. How next to move.

Straight on to another book? The future, as it always does, lies in wait; like a soft, unseen seed. I'm excited to greet it, like a song I want to learn (cheesy AF, as always).

18th

Storm days here for weeks. I am done with it and need some stillness.

I am so tired and overwhelmed with the editing of TP. So ready to put it all in a box and have done with it. What a thing to put oneself and others through, this writing of a life, this excavation.

19th

Treecreeper on the stump outside my desk. Wee bark mousey. Utterly wondrous, oh my heart. What a thing to share the earth with.

Watched so many bullfinches in the rain just now. What colour, what movement.

Second read of *A Ghost in the Throat*. As equally haunting and gorgeous as the first.

Have taken to thinking about writing as a bodily experience. How best I might surrender.

20th

Dublin with L as the blue sky held us close. I had not even nearly realised how much I needed it. Both the place and the person.

21st

John Berger's *The Red Tenda of Bologna*, oh what words! What joy! The section on small, meaningful gifts exchanged between he and his uncle moved me so exceptionally.

When will this heavy rain ease? I am so affected by it this year, for reasons I can't quite put my finger on.

22nd

Traught, the Burren, oh my oh my.

The lichen of a stone-moon.
The absence of a stone-heart.

23rd

Spume, driftwood and a hurley carried in by the storm at Lough Owel.

Met, for the first time, another swimmer there. Talking to her brought the loneliness up from the places in which I try to hide it. No wifi, no signal, too wet to hang about in the data field trying to talk to anyone. Fuck but loneliness is a killer and I don't know how to go about fixing it at all, it seems. I am grateful, of course I am, but I am lonely. I am lonely.

24th
M built me the bookshelf I have long dreamed of.
Things feel much brighter because of it, and I do not mean to sound ingenuine in any way.
Snow, I think, is on its way.

26th
So (heart)sick.
Ghosts of light helping me through, and Karine Polwart's words about the bog and babies; the loss that sinks down deep.

27th
Final push of editing with a yellow candle for courage and a dog that needs her fields.

28th
DONE DONE DONE

29th
Snow sky and sun on alder, after the Inny burst her banks in the night.
There are rivers now where once was only land.
A thin day, moon-flock.

(a dancing, ghost of a day)

I will make of this winter a feathered nook.

Earrach Geamraidh, The Winter Spring

When I awoke on the extra day that this mirrored, mirroring year gave us, it was to winter – come back to me again so fiercely, full of ice – and dancing, piercing light.

The week before, following two unbroken months of harrowing storms, I had held my breath and silently cleared space inside of me – making room for the light of spring. That aul' man of darkness, the king of decay, was on the way out. I was so sure of it I nearly wept with relief. The sodden, lonely fields had had enough of his type – we all had. There had been sun – full, ancient – for only a finger less than a handful of days in the run-up to the final, spectral day of February, so to find the ground outside my rotting, rattling window white and glistening like a dreamed fairy tale – shocked me right to my bones.

Winter – ghost-trace, moon-white, silent as the unimaginable moments after every storm – had arrived back to the laneway. I took the jumper back down from the top shelf, hauled out two pairs of socks, and dragged my tired body outside – into the space created by a day that is neither here nor there, neither real nor imagined. A day more hidden *inside* of, rather than existing *outside* of, time. My first leap year on this isolated laneway, by the central bogland, in the quiet, solitary heart of Ireland. Frost and ice, light and silence, crow-song that echoed all around me like a keen for something not quite lost.

We arrive at the milking barn, the dog leaps ahead of me, as always – to find a shadow-show being played on the old tin sheets, blue as the sky now is, and just as exquisite; just as delicate. Grasses touched by diamonds, making silhouettes of their ethereal forms, as wrens flit from the gaps in a grey stone wall, into the thorns and brambles. The light and the ice are in it together. This thin, spare day exists, it feels − only in the space that lies before my shivery, grateful hands, as I try to record it all on my phone, doing no justice whatsoever to a single drop of it.

Normally we stay here, in this space behind the gate, in front of the stream, for only a minute or two. I circle the perimeters as the dog sniffs the shit of whatever creatures have spent the moonlit hours there. Today, though, the light that has enveloped the milking barn is such that I can see no possibility of leaving it. Its pull on me is like something else that I always thought had no equal or rival. The light that is refracting off freshly born frost, against a backdrop of broken, abandoned machinery made for milking − is calling to me, holding me in place. The light of the 29th of February this year, as if in some surreal and beautiful twist of time and place, is holding me in place like the Atlantic Ocean normally does, even though I am now further away from it than I can ever possibly be on this hinter-land rock − at the very edge-land of Europe.

And so I find myself at the close of February 2020, in an utterly middle place, on a day in betwixt − desperately waiting for spring to take the place of winter − but rapt by the winter's light.

the light the light the light the light; THE LIGHT.

The light that I know I will never quite be able to name, to capture, to hold in my hands. This light whose veins course through this isolated space like a river making its way to the sea. And so, there − on that winter-fabled, frost-guest morning − I start to explore the milking barn, and the outhouses all around of it. Those hidden nooks, beneath fallen trees, and roofs caved in over the passing of the years.

I pass the brown and blue tractor. I pass the brown anchor-like, unidentifiable machine opposite the briars, and I duck into the middle outhouse – the midnight blue starting to come to fruit on the ivy – stepping over glass and thickly crusted dirt, caked into wet rubbish. There is a single vein of that light making its way into the small rectangle. There they sit, two nests, in the left-hand corner, calling out to me – like the sea does – like the light does, even in the dead of winter. Like all gifts, they have come from a place unseen, and a time unknown. I do not speak their language. Still, though, I look. I listen. Still, though, I bring my grateful hands down – in a prayer that needs no name on which to fall.

There are two of them, one is almost half the size of the other, and each has been as skilfully sculpted as the one beside it. The smaller is nestled safely inside the shadow cast by the larger one. They are not a pair, neither are they twinned with one another – yet their twoness, their togetherness, their unity, feels utterly impossible to deny.

I know that they have been crafted
by the repeated movements
of the bodies of birds.

Through the continued, measured actions of their wee fine forms – turning and shaping the material that they themselves have meticulously gathered – sculpting a home for themselves. In this newly fallen, ice-reflecting, vein of light, I look at the two abandoned nests at my feet, as though I am setting eyes upon a kind of beauty that I have never before known. That I will never quite be able to forget. I am not quite sure why but all of a sudden I am crying. I have taken my phone out of my work-jacket, and I am typing what I know for certain are the first words of something – something new, and unnamed (untamed?) – into my notes:

I will make of this winter, a feathered nook.

I step back outside, into the frost that is starting
to disappear like a boneless ghost.

Into the light that is still falling
on the milking barn;

a gossamer dream.

Márta, March

Crow Comes Back Moon
Worm Moon
Snow Crust Moon
Sore Eye Moon
Sap Moon
Wind Strong Moon
Sugar Moon
Lenten Moon
Death Moon
Goose Moon
Moon of the Snowblind

> Half of a life has passed since
> I first began gathering objects.
> Things found in the world outside,
> brought inside, lived alongside.

I've always felt the need – a deep ache, like the seconds before orgasm – to lower my body down to the earth beneath. To sift through whatever was all around of me – sand, shit, soil. To hone in on one thing that called my name, like a lover. On first writing this sentence, I doubted myself, more than momentarily. My brain and body were tired, bone-tired, and so I googled that delicious phrase: *hone in on*. Was it even real or had I imagined it, muddled myself up again? Sometimes words or phrases seem so out of reach of my day-to-day life that I find myself unsure if they even really exist. If I've tangled them all up together like unworn necklaces that I suddenly feel an insatiable desire to wear. I read that the verb *hone* is traceable as far back as the late 1700s, originally: 'to sharpen or smooth with a whetstone', Merriam-Webster shares online. The site seems to think I might be better using the verb *home*, instead, which intrigues me deeply, of course, given that this is the very thing of which I am trying to write.

(Why can't I just let things be? Why am I always chasing the tail of some deeper, mysterious meaning – ever on the search for fate and far-flung sorcery – even in a simple Google search?)

Home can be a verb, it tells me, and I press the namesake button on my screen to italicise. Like pigeons, or a missile, we can home in on an answer, say. Find our way to the destination; the knowing of the thing for which we sought. The online dictionary asks me: Who can blame them, really (these people like me who use *hone* instead of *home*)? Most of us, I am told, only know *home* as a noun.

What do *you* know home as? . . .

Do you feel you even know it at all? Can we write about it, talk about it, fight, fuck or weep over it, without being honest about it? How is it that so many do not, will not, have never once known it? How can we speak about the horror of being unanchored in this shitstorm; without anywhere safe to hide? I don't know how to speak of place any more without acknowledging my privilege. Then there is the knowledge that the words will never be enough, could never be enough. I'm here telling you about a house with a roof and a garden and water and warmth and I am shook with it. With the embarrassment, the shame.

It's not enough.

It's not enough just to know how different it is for so many others.

I know it's far, far from enough.

I sat on the green, paint-chipped trailer by the red and cream milking barn beside my new home for four hours on that extra day of February. I wrote by hand, until all the pale-green ink in my pen had spilled itself out onto the white page:

> *nesting, extra day, lost months, stolen time, flock, flight, storms, flooding, childhood, watching the crows gathering sticks on Bute until I missed my ferry, flatness, curves, hollow, frost, ghosts, roots, lightlightlightlightlightlight, solitude, LIGHT*

I wrote for that extra day and for the three days that followed it – the first three of March. Words that felt like I'd bled them out, outlandish though that sounds. I had a migraine so bad it reminded me of my very first migraine; convinced the world was coming to an end. On the 4th I went back to other words

– paid work that had deadlines – words that had a concrete shape, and that followed a clear line. Unlike those new words. Those other words that arrived – unbidden – not quite fully formed, in the frosty light of a milking barn, a space that is not even nearly mine, an abandoned, borrowed place. On the 7th I sent off a review for an exquisite gift of a book – Sara Baume's *Handiwork* – the last thing that I would ever write before the whole world as we know it changed shape and colour. My journal for the 8th of March would show a dark, fog-grey line if I allowed myself to reread it, something about there being a gap between the known and the unknown, and no light with which to navigate.

It took less than a week, after the nests, to sense that something was not right in the world outside the lane, a world we only glimpsed in scraps. If enough signal could be had to search the news, we read enough to realise that the winter had come back. That we would not now be emerging, not travelling out from our new centre, in search of places beyond the island's boggy middle. That we all, in fact, would be remaining where we lay, in those parts of land we'd spent the long-drawn winter, for a spell it was too early, then, to forecast.

The days since the 8th of March have been steeped in the full, unimaginable debris – of a storm that showed no sign of arriving, that shows no indication of letting up. At the exact point of the year, in many parts of the UK and Ireland, when the actual, measurable, recordable, nameable storms looked as though they were on their way out, a pandemic – unlike almost everything we have ever known before – arrived.

Spring came and found us in behind closed doors – isolated and alone, as if we had begun a second winter.

Every single year, when the ending of winter comes, I forget how fully I can be tricked by the light. Spring always seems to be just *there*, and then comes the wind and the rain – the sleet and the snow – the light that I know can only be the light of winter. The uncertain, tumultuous weather that marks the passage from winter to spring on these islands often alights with us at the ending of March and can stay right into April. We often witness a winter relapse, the embers of the darkest season not quite gone out; tended to – brought back to life – plunging us right back into the depths of the cold.

When the spring equinox came this year it felt almost surreal how bright, how warm – how spring spring spring – it was. Then, two days later, on the 22nd, we found ourselves at the start of 'The Borrowed Days' – where I am from, at least. In Scotland and in the south of Ireland, the borrowed days mostly refer to the last two days of March and the first two of April, but in the north of Ireland we have a tale of nine days, borrowed from April – to kill and skin an old brindled cow.

'Borrow': 'To take or receive something with the implied intention of returning it to its owner or the place where it *belongs*. One can be "Living on borrowed time".'

'To introduce words or ideas from another person or language into your own.'

In *Handiwork*, a book I hope never to keep too far from my hands, Baume writes of migration in a way that I have never thought of it before, and I cannot shake it from out of my insides: 'There has to be one who rises first' – talking of the individual bird, amongst an entire flock, the one that makes that first move. 'There has to be one who rises first.' I hope, and I trust, that she will not mind if I borrow these dancing, beautiful words – only for a wee while (or perhaps for ever).

When W sends me help to identify the moth in my lockdown kitchen, attaching photos of other moths she has taken – what she is really doing is sharing her hope. She is reminding me – in the third week of isolation – of the night she took my picture in the bustling backstreets of Bristol, my jacket completely covered in moths, in a December that feels three years ago instead of the months it really is. She is saying: There are so many miles between us right now. Still, though, I see your moth. Still, though, you see mine. There are still moths, my friend is saying. There are still moths, and we still love them. She is saying: Remember the resilience of small things. No matter how delicate you feel today, you have the wings to span vast oceans.

There has to be one who rises first.

Sometimes, moments come in our lives when it is very difficult – almost impossible – to return things to the people and the places in which they are deemed as 'belonging', as per the definition of 'borrowing'.

In this wee stone cottage sit, in an array of odd locations, seven library books that I have no idea when I will be able to return. Words I have written by hand sit on top of the desk my love has fashioned me; words that I should be carrying with me next week, across the sea, to Devon – for a project two years in the making, now rescheduled by the artist for next year, in the hope that this will all pass soon. I have a friend who is held in Italy with her new partner, with no clue when she will return to Spain. Maybe when she eventually does, it will be to collect the rest of her belongings and take them to the new place she may have already begun to belong to. She is planting seeds there, in the place she found herself when this storm hit. On every surface she can find. I know when I see her hands working in this way that she, herself, is putting down roots.

There are seeds in this house that should already be in the soil outside – soil that should already have had all the roots and broken glass removed by a loaned digger that is in a yard, patiently waiting; until who knows when. I don't really know where those waiting seeds belong right now. They are on top of a bench my partner made for us to sit on in the garden. The bench is made from parts of salvaged decking, built by the previous owner, that rotted almost right through in the decade that the house lay empty. I fell through that decking, on the autumn equinox, and took it as the house's way of asking me if I was really meant to be there. Here in this cottage inherited by the person I love, in a place to which I have absolutely no ties.

This year, on the spring equinox – after two full days of my anxious, fearful howling, hours given over to weeping like a baby – my partner took the rest of that decking and built a bird-table. The day before, as we'd made our way as quickly through the supermarket as we could – masked and gloved – he'd bought fat-balls and nuts, seeds of various colours and sizes. He didn't say anything, he just put them in the trolley, on the conveyor, in the bag, in the van, into the feeders, onto the table he had built them.

When the birds came, I cried.

I cried and cried and cried because of grief.

Grief I have already spent far too much time, energy and ink on.

I cried because of the loss, the fear, the worry. I cried for people and places – things and realities – that I both know and do not know. I cried because, yes, there is such loss, sorrow and grief but oh my, there is still so much hope left, despite it all.

And I cried when the birds came because I finally felt safe, somehow.

There were so many of them, of so many different varieties. There were so many of them, and they squabbled and fought, bullied and dilly-dallied. They ate and they left. There were so many of them, and they came to our small house, to where the rotted deck used to be, and they ate the food we gave them. They were golden and black with red heads. They were brown, they were burnt orange. They were green and yellow, green and green, blue and green, black and grey, pink and pewter, black and shiny. They were gifts.

When my partner built that table and bought food for those birds, what he was saying was: Yes the world as we know it has changed beyond all words but there are things that need no words. There are still things that we can do. Look at all those birds we never knew that there could be.

He was saying that sometimes things break and smash and rot, and then the parts left over can be hammered into something new. What my partner was saying was that it takes so little, so very little indeed, to call the winged, coloured things down from out of the sky. There is very little that we need to do that can change our days so fully, so completely – one day at a time. He is saying that there is much that we cannot control – much suffering that we would all give our all to stop, to ease, to undo – but that we are trying our best. We are trying our best to keep each other safe.

When the bird builds her nest in the tree, in the shed, in the eaves, in the dovecote, in the car engine, in the wellie, in the outhouse, she is not placing her trust in the space onto which she builds. When the bird builds her nest – her safe, feathered nook – she places trust in the fine, repeated movements of her own feathered body.

'There has to be one who rises first.'
WE RISE.

1st

Long-tailed tits in the orchard this morning.
Buttercups and wrens, too.
Blue in the sky, and I am so grateful for it.
Blackbird in the rushes.
The pussy willow has opened its whiteness up to the world
in the night.
It feels, finally, like things might be all right.

Have begun to write about two things, over and over, it seems:
light and solitude.
I have never been anything other than solitary but this winter
solitude has made a home of me so unstoppably, almost tenderly,
as a bird shapes her nest.
(Writing a life is an odd old thing.)

2nd

Awoke to frost, like a dream scene. The dog is like a wee puppy,
so full of joy.
Sabhaircín, the first primrose I have seen this year.
Sent a photo to lovely Z, who adores them.

3rd

Edwyn Collins up full-pelt in the morning sun.
The sound of spring, at last.
Frost all around once more.
Sligo. Larks of the sky. Cliffs of the sea. Veins of the light.

Crow moon
Snow sky
Solitary winter

The moon – on the wane – a cold, winter, mourning white,
looks down, and I can hear the song. I can hear the gaps

between the notes, I can hear the dips and dives. I can hear the space that has been carved for me – for you. I can hear the still point where I know we all must meet.

4th

A lush run up the laneway, then straight into the field for a walk with the dog.

When I ran past A's farmyard she shouted, in the most gorgeous way, 'You're fabulous,' and I realise there might be nothing more I want in all the world than for a woman like A to think I am fabulous (and to say it).

Straight after, the most exquisite murmuration swooped below the moon, and I could feel the tears running down my sweaty red face (and it felt like that was the first time in months that I'd known I was alive, alive, alive).

Something about today feels so full of hope.

5th

First goldfinch on the feeder this morning.

The sun is out(ish).

Editing first book and first steps towards second at the desk M fashioned me from an old plank off a ship. Fuck am I grateful for a space of my own, one at which I imagine I can hear the keening of the sea, one at which I imagine I can nurture the words.

Do right by them. Let them find their own way.

6th

Reviewed *Inventory* by Darran Anderson and am changed by his words. 'How might it be possible to . . . thread bone onto soul . . . a presence in the shape of an absence.' I am shattered by the way he shares his truth, put back together again differently, for certain.

This evening's run: wrens, blackbirds, starlings making for murmuration beneath a pink sky holding a waning moon. Daffodils at the top of the lane and buttercups in the boreen making me reach, again, for the yellow section in *The Grassling* – perhaps the most perfect piece of writing ever.

8th
Thinking today of all the women who have been wounded by the women in their pasts. Women who, in spite of this deep ache, are so good to the women in their lives, creatures of a very particular kind of light. International Women's Day. Sometimes the best days are the hardest of all.

10th
Spent hours arranging stones into a line at the top of my desk. I am unsure why, and as equally unsure why I feel the need to write this down (but I do, and must respect that urge, I feel).

Tonight's run: pale blue sky full of longing, blackbirdsblackbirdsblackbirds and pink veins of healing light.

13th
Tonight's run: bullfinches, a song thrush and a single poppy head blowing in the close-of-day breeze.

14th
W. told me today is moth day.
Sarah Gillespie's *Moth* book is published. She writes so well of the act of looking – really looking – as a delicate act of kindness and solidarity. The natural world as part of us, a part we must protect.
Greenfinch on the feeder. Moved so deeply by this and unsure why. Not just the fact I have never really seen one before but something that runs deeper than this. The colour, the movement,

the way the morning light caught in its feathers as M chopped the wood before breakfast. It all feels so heartbreakingly beautiful, tender.

15th
Larks of the sky.
Gorse of the bog.
Bees of the pine.

Tonight's run: pussy willow, thrushes and pewter clouds above storm-orange sky.

16th
Stood at the sycamore tree in the high field as cancellation after cancellation of work came into my email. I don't want to worry about this, there is so much else to think about (but I am scared).

17th
Bought the last of the shamrock in Aldi. Lit a green candle. We still must mark the days that mattered to us before, unsure of the shapes these things might take as we make our way onwards.
M came in from the shed with the most beautiful object I have ever set eyes upon. A stool, carved, from leftover wood, for me. On a day spent constantly on the verge of crying, this felt the most loving act of which I have ever been on the receiving end. I learn from this man so much it is almost unthinkable how life would be right now without him.

18th
Woke from a dream where I remembered halfway through that I was sober and in the dream I cried with relief and the tears stained my dress.

19th
Morning
Did I just carry my ache into the belly of an ancient limestone lough?

And did it hold me close?
And did I float like a thing remade?

Evening
cocoon / shedding / remembering / emerging
(There is a light out there that wasn't there before this arrived.)

20th
Vernal Equinox
This morning, wakening halfway between six and seven, running out to the gate in front of the cottage I find the field bathed in amber-red glow, all dappled light and delicate urgency. Thoughts return, firstly, to half a year ago – the autumn equinox, when we awoke facing that very same field in our van at exactly such a sunrise. Later that day we found out we would safely and legally be allowed to move into our home. Between that day and the winter solstice, M worked so hard for us to make the place liveable, and now we find ourselves here, on a sunny spring equinox, in a vastly changed world – one that feels so eerily unchanged, though, too. Soft red sunrises, partnerships, skeletal trees. A laneway bathed in veins of light chaotic with birdsong. A world full of deep, unsettling uncertainty and worry but as equally full of solidarity and kindness, beauty.

An odd, hard few days. Abandonment issues are a headfuck. So weepy. I'm certain I'm not the only one. We are, none of us, going to be the same when we come out of this. Feels like we are learning how to be human again, harrowing but essential work.

21st

Treecreeper keeping me company as I work outside, by the milking shed, imagining a different time than this one.

22nd

Mother's Day – found a perfect antler in the bottom field. Ache for a baby so deep as to keep me from sleep.

23rd

Sat in grass beside milking barn – dog at my feet – long-tailed, great and blue tits calling in the trees beneath a ghost-white sky. Considering what it means to be listening right now in this vastly changed and changing world. Of what it means to open ourselves up to all that comes towards us: chant; scream; song; keen; whimper – and how we might learn to really *hear*. When the world has, in many spaces, grown more and more quiet; the outdoors feels a riot of sound. Some we haven't heard for quite some time; if ever.

And then, looking, too, observing – trying to really *see* – feels so important right now. Like we could learn so much from such a gentle act. Of small and quiet things. What does it all say to our place in this broken, beautiful world? To our role? To the need and the ache – the suffering and the sorrow – the delicate, terrifying act of being alive? What can we do to support those with the deepest ache, the vastest loss? What do we need to unlearn to make room for what we've forgotten? Compassion, kindness, care, goodness, solidarity, selflessness. Nothing feels set in stone any longer.

The earth shifts beneath our feet.

All we can do right now is stop.

Breathe.

(Try to breathe.)

To make every step and breath we take into an act of compassion. We are asked to cocoon. When we emerge will we have been sculpted? Will we feel more human? I feel like we've been self-isolating here since December – through geography, weather and circumstance – so this all feels so eerily 'normal'. I have made the circle in which I move much smaller this year, tighter.

Now I watch it fold in on itself once more.

Smaller, tighter again.

Smaller than ever before.

25th

They closed the lake, the only thing that's kept me calm so far. Unsure what the weeks ahead might look like, given how desperately I've relied on the cold water this year to get me through various layers of grief, but others are far worse off. We must look out for one another, including our own selves.

First swim in bog river.

Mud & reeds. Coots & whooper swans. Concrete & willow.

The first red admiral of the season and fuck am I grateful.

26th

Mothlight, as always.

Reading Annie Dillard on sycamores after I spent the week writing about one.

Speedwell Veronica. Celandine. A solitary peacock butterfly in the milking barn.

And bumble bees. So many bumble bees.

Tonight's run: a vast, low, ancient red sun setting – leaving a dash of pink above pewter trees and singing hedgerows. A whisper of a newly born moon – soft and silent – beneath white Venus. Home to fire-walking. Clapping our gratitude for those we cannot see, echoing through the trees.

27th
Pink morning.
Awoke to an image: my name written in the sand by C on my favourite beach after she swam at sunrise. Moved me too much to try to word.
They haven't closed Lough Derravaragh so I swam there, swans at all angles, as the sun hid behind dove-grey clouds.

28th
A moth beneath a new moon and Venus, at the tail end of March.
Locked down, as of midnight last night, to within 2 kilometres of the cottage.
The softest, most silent sunset I think I've ever seen.

30th
Yesterday: blue sky above golden grasses. Skylarks & snipe.
Falling asleep by the stove, only to wake up as the thin, white moon edged towards the top of the window, where the treecreeper once was.
Baked scones & banana loaf for A, who is cocooning. Left on doorstep. Would have given almost anything to see her.

31st
We left it, as advised, until it was utterly essential to leave home to find the van won't start.
Gathered dandelions and baby blackberry leaves for salad.
Run today was clunky, hard and achy. There were wagtails though, and maybe wild iris.
And a wing of beautiful, mottled feathers.

I cannot get away, these last weeks, of thinking about how we choose to spend our days.

Of our rituals.

Ritual finds form through the assumption that it is a means of really knowing something. Religious ceremony and personal rites of passage fill my thoughts. The gentle, insistent act of repeating. How it creates equilibrium between the small & the vast, the seen & unseen, the self & other, the part & the whole. We build myths (which are really just houses). Dwelling places built of the bones left behind from stories. We fill the gaps in the walls with ritual. We insulate it with objects.

Ritualistic to their very core, objects are both mothered by and mother to individual habits, customs, practices. Objects make us do a plethora of things simply by their existence. We might buy, steal, make, move, paint, break, mend. We might dream of, hope for, throw from a height, adorn our bodies with. We might beg, borrow or steal.

A particular object might obsess us, repel us, pleasure us, bind us, separate us. It might bring us into being . . . or carry us when we've reached the journey's end. An object might remain with us for every given moment in between. We might gather, order, compare, record, alter. We might do all of this or none of it at all. Mostly, though, we choose to hold them. To keep them. To clasp them and to keep them close. We *choose* the objects of our lives – and in this choosing we offer something of ourselves to these things with which we share our days.

What do we give to the objects in our lives?

> We give them worth.
> We place value on them.

I gather objects from places that I see as *mattering* to me.
I carry them, then, into dwelling places because I have fooled myself, over the space of a lifetime, that in doing so I come closer to the object, the places, the self.
What on earth ever made me imagine my identity so intimately interwoven with the physical world? This landscape of stuff and matter?

What would it mean to leave them, these objects?

> To walk away.
> To carry on along the path.

To put the key in the door and walk through it, empty-handed. To knock the walls down, let the light creep around every corner and drip down into every nook and cranny.

What might it mean to hold nothing in your hands?

> To choose
> nothing in
> the place of
> something?

If objects are ritual, then what would it mean to leave these objects?
What would it mean to leave these objects, these rituals; these stories? This house?

Seeing [an object] as itself means removing it from the flow
of time, returning it to the mute fire from which it came.

Luis Sagasti

I have found myself, in these last weeks, thinking of objects.
And I have found myself, in these last weeks, thinking of geese.

Thinking, rather, about an old storybook of geese.

There were exactly twelve of them and every single one of
them was wild.

There were twelve wild geese, *fadó fadó*, long long ago.

That's not how it all began, though. We all know the first
sentence is never the beginning, really. It never was. I doubt it
ever will be, to be fair.

The start, if we can even really trace the roots of anything
– let alone old Irish lore – sees us with two old monarchs on
our hands. Sure it's always a king and a queen, am I right? It
never begins with you, or with me. Even though that's the real
story, every single time.

(Over and over and over I want to know about *you*. I want
to know about me.)

Anyway, the king and the queen were living in Ireland. They
had twelve sons. Always sons, of course. There was snow. Always,
there is snow. There are no grey areas in these old stories. It
is always black and white. The coal in the fire. The eyes of the
bear. The ebony hair of the woman at hand. The swan with
human song; the rose in the walled garden; the shine of the
moon on a lake . . . So, yes, in this story there is white to
begin with, and that white is the driven snow.

In this story the black is a raven, velvety and as still as stopped
time. When I first typed the raven line, I wrote 'stooped time'
instead of stopped, and it lingered for quite some time. The
error rang like a stolen bell.

How might stooped time show itself?

How would it look and act?
How would it hold itself as a trace inside our memory?
Thin as willow, bent over itself, eyes always down to the ground.
Making an old crone of our lived days.

(Time; you funny, unsettling creature.)

In this story the raven is dead: stopped, stooped time.
In this story the queen is not only a wife – for the king is
never merely a husband, you understand – but she is a mother,
too. This queen is the mother of twelve strapping sons. The
queen is *not* the mother of even one single, solitary daughter.
There are no princesses at the start of this old, old tale. She
finds herself, the mother-queen, on this winter's morn, watching
blood seep out of a once-scavenging, once-folkloric bird.

O! how the red and the black and the white make a creaturely
object.
How they swim together on her insides and make a person.
A small person.
A person with cheeks as red as the blood, with skin as white
as the snow, with hair as black as the dead raven's wing.
A child-person.
A girl-child.
A daughter.

The old queen had never felt her ache move so freely, so
forcefully, so furiously, before that winter's day. The old queen
was a liar: she had simply never seen her desire made as real,
was all. Never before had she seen her desire lie in the snow
before her feet. Her unborn creature, her unborn child, her

unborn daughter. Right there before her on a snowy mid-winter's day. Ready to take shape, to stand up, to dance.

Her dancing daughter.

I am a liar too. The old queen was not old. She was still 'of an age'. She still gathered up her hopes for a daughter at the moon moments of her month. When the next month came around, as red as raven blood. She took back out her hopes, polished them like brass trinkets, and put them away until the bright white circle above her was full. This was how the not-too-old queen had resigned herself to spending her years. Watching as the ache in her grew fatter; wishing her belly would do the same, cursing her insides as if they were a bag of filthy parlour-rats. And so the young, tired, beautiful mother stood, eyes green as ivy, hair light as flax, heart heavy as thunder, and listened as words gushed out of her like those beating, bulging afterbirths. She had no control over it all, over any of it, least of all what she said on that lonely snowy day.

'O! If I had a daughter with skin as white as that snow, with cheeks as red as that blood, with hair as black as that raven's wing; I'd give my twelve sons away for her!'

A window was open, but no one was around to hear.

Sure, lookit, the words were hardly out of her mouth when up comes a red cloak with a small woman attached to it.

'Well, Queenie, you will have your wish. Before twelve months have been and gone you will have her, your heart's desire – but the day she comes along you will lose those strapping, laughing, farting, living sons.'

Well my oh my did the queen dance. Did she laugh and weep and relish in the future like a seed in wait.

And sure wasn't the king only delighted to see his lover laughing again.

He'd mind the lads, don't worry. His boys would come to no harm at all.

We remember, of course, that it always involves walls . . .

A whole room of them, a whole wing of them, a whole castle of walls.

To keep the boys in. To keep the world out.

Now then.

Back to the object at hand, the raven at the queen's foot.

Back to the coveting of, the want of – the *let me hold, let me have, let me keep* of it all.

Back to the object of the young woman's desire.

The child-person, the girl-child, the daughter.

She came.

And, indeed, she was as fair as the driven snow.

And, indeed, her lips were red as fresh blood.

And, indeed, her hair was as black as a raven.

As the feathery wing of a dead raven, in fact.

And she had only just arrived before the queen loved her, this object of her desire, this raven-child, more than all the other things in the world.

And she had only just arrived before the whole feasting, celebrating kingdom watched twelve wild geese fly high – above the room, above the wing, above the castle, above every wall the king could build.

Twelve wild sons.

Twelve strapping, laughing, farting, living sons.

Turned to birds.

There is so much more, you understand, to this achy, ancient tale.

There is a daughter grown older, a hag of truth, a journey to a vast, dark wood.
   There is a house built of objects.
   There is twelve of everything.
   There is a bog & bog-cotton & weaving.
   There is a woman forced into silence, as always.
   There is a great fire on which to burn her.
   There are twelve wild geese made into brothers, again . . .

         . . . All of this to tell you that the geese left.

I stood, mud underfoot,
as they honked their departure overhead:
a disharmony of feather.

Aibreán, April

Pink Moon
Seed Moon
Planter's Moon
Awakening Moon
Breaking Ice Moon
Sprouting Grass Moon
Budding Trees Moon
Green Grass Moon
Moon of the Red Grass Appearing
Moon When the Streams Are Again Navigable
Paschal Moon
Fish Moon
Frog Moon
Hare Moon
Egg Moon

For as long as I've been able to name the days & months – to observe their colourful, untameable lexicon, the aching cycle of seasons – I have struggled with the month of April. It sneaks up on me like the name of someone long lost in the soft pink dawn of morning. It's like the shipping forecast on the radio in those moments when sleep will not come . . . I know its beauty is there, right in front of me but (for reasons too sore and echoey to give voice to) I am unable to access it. I find myself cowering silently instead – not yet able to see the green growth that unfurled, noiselessly, inside the winter's darkling grip.

I know that for this corner of the planet April means the land's shift towards an unknowable horizon; a season, like a place, that we can never quite pin down. Spring – *well* I know – is supposed to be a time of new beginnings, of hope, of light. But the thing is, life does not always tick along in the way we might will it to, and many of us find ourselves, at points of the year's circle when we imagine we *should* feel this, or that, feeling another way entirely.

The most difficult things I have experienced have all happened in that fourth month, things that spoke to me in no way of rebirth or joy. Things that spoke instead of loss, of endings, of grief that stung and bit. From a young age I have been the kind of person that wills away the spring. Its transitional, slippery nature has always felt a bit too close to the bone for me. I'm distrustful of its liminal, hidden ways.

This is an April – on both sides of the equator – unlike many of us have ever known. Many of us have sensed, for a stretch of varying lengths before now, that things were shifting in the outside world. I had felt something amiss on this isolated laneway, in the very heart of Ireland, just before Laethanta na Riabhaí, those 'borrowed, skinning days' that mark the end of March and the beginning of April in old Celtic lore. The news is confusing. It grows harder to decipher with each passing day, and the outside world's chaos mirrors changes going on beneath my own skin. After three and a half decades constantly on the move, from one rented space to another, a lifetime spent running with all that I could carry in my arms, I have found somewhere I know, if I want to, I'll be able to *stay*.

As soon as we locked down, my lover set at the brambles and thorns in the wild space behind the house with any tool he could get his hands on, clearing and making space. Having never lived anywhere for any proper time, I have no idea what to do in a garden. If I'm honest, I was reticent at the start. If I'm truly honest, I was terrified.

How does someone learn to stay?

To give their body over to a small stretch of land?
What does it mean to tend to a garden, when so much pain has been inflicted in our world and our land?

We aren't alone in throwing ourselves into this small stretch of land we can suppose to call 'our own'. My social-media threads are full to bursting with people placing their hands into the soil, trying to quieten down the cacophony of the unfolding news. It feels as clichéd as any of us can really imagine, but as the world outside becomes more and more scary, rather than hiding inside, we seem to be entering deeper into the earth's hidden folds. A funny old mix of gratitude and guilt swims inside my belly, and again I don't think I'm alone. That some are stuck, lonely, surrounded only by bricks and strangers, breaks my heart afresh each day. What gives me the right to stand among birds and brand-new life, green and hopeful?

I have less than no clue what to do. The when, the how, the where of it all. Despite the excitement it overwhelms me – in ways I find too hard to really talk about.

After weeks spent raising the handful of seeds I'd been lucky enough to get hold of, one freak storm lifted my flimsy plastic 'greenhouse' and hurled it against the boiler. Practically everything I'd nurtured into being was lost. I posted the pictures of the scene on Instagram, seeking some kind of response from people I mostly haven't even met. I could make no sense of it: the obsession & the torment, the desire & the peace it all brought, somehow. The responses were all from women. Some I 'knew' already, many I didn't. Every single one of them was soothing, encouraging: full of goodness. And full of something else, too. Full of sharing. Lettuce & radish seeds arrived from Bournemouth with love and with crockery. Wild-flower seeds for the bees from Brighton, deadly nightshade and an art deco postcard from France, cosmos and a handmade ring from Bristol, honesty from Orkney.

So much more than seeds are being passed between us. We are sharing, from our tiny, backlit screens – in various degrees of lockdown and of heartache – tips & images, resources & timeframes; our gardens feel almost womb-like. Places we might feel held. Spaces outside of the normal confines of place or time. Being there, no matter what we lose, no matter what blows we and the garden suffer, is giving so many of us a means of feeling buoyed. A way to feel set free, and so much less alone than we really are.

I read, again and again, how people now recognise the garden as somewhere that holds the potential to imagine things coming along, things they might long have taken as impossible. How it might hold you close, as you realise – through bone-achingly tiring, rhythmical work – that you feel differently about things than you had before you began.

Many of us have carried much, so much, into the hidden places within our gardens in these last months. For an unfathomably long period of time, the only other person I have set eyes upon is the one I live with. But I feel less alone than I have for most of my life.

There is a kind of grief that brings us closer together,
that calls us to action: that clears space for hope.

Much is and will be lost in these uncertain times. But there is so much we can still look after. There is still so much that we can give.

I walk, twice per day, the same two fields. Over and over and over.

I have become mildly obsessed with drawings of moths.

Those of other people – real artists – as well as my own.

In general, I have become more drawn to image than to words.

I am not sure why. I have started, after so many years away from it, to paint again.

I convince myself, for almost a week, that I am done with words.

That there is no point to them.

Then I waken to find a small bird perched on our yellow front door and I see it carries, in its fine beak, all the words I could ever hope to write and I am right back in it again, in the flow that I know I really always want to be carried along with.

I paint the Seed Pink Moon.

This is a time to sow the seeds for all that we hope will flourish in the season of fertility and growth ahead. I try to write of my need, my desire – but I fail. How would I ever begin to try to voice those hopes? These things I long for so badly it makes me feel queasy, seasick? I know it's biology, this instinct I try to steer myself away from, but it hurts, it hurts so badly. With every year that passes by I know I am growing older, growing into a woman that isn't mothering, that might never, and the ache feels too much to even try to speak of. Time is playing tricks on me these last months and I feel cheated (and selfish in ways I cannot even process). I am sickened by this feeling, by this sense of uncontrollable loss. Sometimes I wonder if we should sit down, M and I, and find a way to make sense of it. Find answers to questions I can't even verbalise. That I hoped, for years, would go the fuck away.

This moon is named after moss pink, or wild ground phlox, the pink flowers that bloom in early spring. Remember when we used to follow the seasons, the harvest, the cycles, the moons, the tides? When it wasn't all sliced up, perfectly, from the whole, into parts that feel mechanical, forced, so wildly out of place and pace?

1st

Drew, with forest-green ink, M as he slept by the stove. Can't quite get over how lucky I am to be by his side some days. The last while would have devastated me without his quiet, calm strength.

2nd

Van completely off the road. Will make for an interesting time, I imagine, given the circumstances.
Have never struggled as badly with my sobriety than today. Thinking of all those in the same boat, picturing them carrying lanterns, us guiding each other through, etc.

3rd

Reading Ellena Savage's exquisite *Blueberries*. 'It is the writing within a life that gives moments of reprieve from solitude.' Yes, oh yes.

4th

Discovered Tim Robinson has died. A writer who has always compelled me to consider how best to *be* in a place. 'I am too restless to sink into the moment for more than a moment at a time. Horizons beckon, and what's beyond them.' Must write to R.

Pussy willow so glorious this morning as to bring me close to tears. It feels like I have never really seen it before, somehow, like I never really knew how to look at it to really see. Worried I might be being dragged under by the spring this year, by its chaos and its heady mystery.

5th

Rain. Home from the bog and straight into bed. Reading by candlelight. I needed this comfort more than I can say. This stillness.

6th

> The first swallow,
> In the soft, fierce light,
> At Granard.

Started the final edits on TP.
This year, of darkness and of light, has altered my internal landscape for ever.

7th

Awoke to frost, light, and the sound of a solitary greenfinch.
Full sun, full pink seed moon.
Have only noticed this year that buds always appear white before turning green.
Unsure why this feels such an awfully big deal. How it feels full of inexplicable and reverent mystery.
Editing whilst wearing a ceramic whale brooch.
Hope always to make room for the small alongside the vast.
Sowed broad beans, mixed beets, Californian poppies, cornflowers and butternut squash.

8th

Full sun.
Sowed seeds into every empty pot we could find or make.
Felt so grateful I wept in the early evening sun. Melancholy feels an incongruous gift, sometimes.

9th

Trip for essentials. Garda checkpoint at top of laneway.
Harrowing.
Home to the most thoughtful box of food from L, which made me cry in front of the calendar which has an image of women farming, because I am growing to understand that love in its purest form is nourishment.

Full sun which waned in the afternoon.
Sowed evening stock beside the corn.
Then – aubergine, sweet basil, rocket, chives, thyme, cauliflower, beans and sweet pepper.

10th
Day 33 of lockdown.
Sat by stove waiting for crumble to be ready.
Have written during it all, somehow, but have struggled with these pages this week for some reason. Today felt an important one to mark, in many ways.
Good Friday. 22 years to the day since the Good Friday Agreement.
The start of Easter properly, a time I've long struggled with.
Awoke this morning, and when M was treating the dog's ears, realised I'd had my first normal dream for over a month.
An old French house. A long corridor. Awoke early to write in a room that was mine alone. Beneath the gap, at the threshold, an enchanting, sculpted white moth, bowed in on itself in a foetal position. Like the one in the kitchen a few weeks back. As I glanced, went closer: not a moth at all but a small white owl chick. Close to dying. Breathed life back into its lungs. Took it out – into the brightly breaking day – finally finding rest in the knowledge that it was going to make it through.

Always with moths.
Moths that aren't real.
That aren't dead.
That aren't moths.

Always with things from troubling places, in the middle of dark nights, carried into the day.

Walked along the stream. In the reeds I watched, for the first time, the birds I've been trying to identify through their call alone. They are reed buntings. Stood with a sense of stillness I'm not sure I've ever really experienced before today. Spent much of last night thinking how I always go into the wild on Easter weekend, normally. Promised myself I'd not give space, even on a page, to the events of the Easter weekend I first ran from a home; enough already. All this is to say I'm craving rawness. Release.

Instead, I gather objects. Remind myself that I, too, am a thing worth being cherished. .

No gathering today. Nowhere to go.

I hold, instead, the objects I already have close, closer still.

Morning swim at Lough Lene to ease the ache & fog.

So much emotion in the milking barn.

Red admirals landing on a sleeping hound, swallows all encircling me, and writing about Heaney & his ripples. Then Leo Varadkar quoted him – wintering now so we may summer anywhere, etc. It's all so much, so very much. Too much.

Deep feeling, deep letting go.

More sowing (nothing else for it).

A gloaming walk. Gathering Easter branches when I caught, at the edge of my vision, at the entrance to the stream at the woods – the white, exact, dream-object shape: a skull.

Deeply, vastly moved. Less than a kilometre from the house, in the fifth week of such isolation, delicate, carved objects still find their way onto my path, and fuck am I fiercely grateful.

Badger.

The whole shape of its form is, when viewed straight on, the exact shape of the moth-owl.

Bent in on itself.

Hollow space.

Consider the idea, briefly, that I have dreamed this gift into being, somehow; then cop myself on.
Hope, always, to feel this level of gratitude. Never to slump back down into *poor wee me*.

Nightfall.
Past my ear: the buzzing of swift, small wings.
A black moth – too quick to try to identify – closing Good Friday with the exact opposite.

12th
Easter Sunday

Started by rereading Mark Strand's 'The Coming of Light' – unadulterated beauty.

Eggs shared in bed. Grey, wet day which cleared mid-afternoon. A walk up the parallel laneway. Garlic mustard. Mare's tail. Bluebells in the old, wrecked cottage, first I've seen this year due to lockdown. Daffodils and Queen Anne's lace gathered for the table. Met, on the way back from the 1930s keep, A & J. J loved the brownies.
Home to editing and lovely dinner. Thinking back, although I try so hard not to, on all the other Easters that went before. A shares a birthday with Heaney, a fact that moves me something drastic.

13th
Faint half-moon in the blue.
Heaney's birthday.
I will feel, always, the loss of him.
Lots of gardening after a fine walk. Swallows in the sky, reed buntings where they should be, and joy in myself.

Blue tit flew straight into window. The trees, we note, are reflected so perfectly in the glass. Must place shapes on it to try to prevent from happening again.

It clung to the stone on the wall, then its whole body – neck and head firstly – made as though to topple to the ground below. M said to hold it, so – without touching its body – I caught and cradled it in the safe nook of my blue merino jumper as though it were a nest. We waited, watching as its heartbeat calmed down. Its eyes closed, then reopened, making contact with mine, its beads locked with my ones, blue for its black. I laid it upright – claws able to support it – just beneath the feeders. We waited, and a moment came when I thought it dead. We stayed until – flash-like – it darted away, up into the spring air.

14th

Willow warbler.

Chiffchaff.

Peacock butterfly.

A pair of reed buntings.

Swallows that will not be captured.

Garden cleared by J.

Editing most of day in milking barn, the parts about M at the beginning of TP.

J gave me gorse and redcurrant bushes.

Best-looking sourdough yet.

JS received her package and is very moved by it.

Found, in the field by the barn, the remainder of a collared-dove egg.

So beautiful, so white; so full of spring.

Skeletons in the beautiful blue sky (there is no other adjective for it today I'm afraid . . .)

So many birds.

So much light.

15th
M's anniversary.
Remembering the version of her I felt safe around.
Grieving through light.
I started TP just hours before news of her death reached me.
Today I'll hand in what I hope to be an almost ready MS.
A cabbage white and willow warbler helping with final push.
I'll go, then, to tell the bees about her. About her laughter and
her beauty, as well as the darkness.

16th
Cannot convey how it feels to be sowing seeds in the earth
right now.
How it feels to watch them reach for the light, grow towards
it, in this moment of such disquieting uncertainty.
I struggle to find the words to speak of it.
Am going to try to write a book about it, someday.

Breacfhéileacán Coille, Speckled Wood

Sunday

When I arrive back from the bog, soaked to the bone, shaken to the core, my lover asks for facts, always facts, he needs, you see, to find the way back to the beginning. By the time enough signal could be found for me to ring him, I'd already made it halfway back to our home. He ran across the lower field, thick with dancing grasses and dipping swallows, to meet me. Home – dripping icy water and adrenalin – to the stove, and to tea. To finding words, somehow, for a wordless, ineffable thing.

It was a Sunday, that soaking, shivery day, 24 hours after an injured breacfhéileacán coille – a speckled wood butterfly, spent an hour on my hand. Only one day since I stayed with it, and it with me, beneath a canopy of ash and hawthorn, light bleeding through like poetry; like some trickery, or relic. I'd thought it dead, at moments, we both had, and my lover had gone back about his business, making new things out of broken things, bird feeders from rotted decking, bookshelves from bits leftover from other times. He was not willing to let this changed, confusing time drag him into idleness or despair. The only things close to us on this laneway are horses & cows, birds & insects, badgers & foxes, rats & (maybe) pine martens, a single Irish newt & a bog full of silence. We've not struggled to keep our physical distance – harrowing though it's been.

It was, that Sunday, the start of the eighth week we had spent at home. We have so little signal here, at this the last dwelling before the land turns into bog, and so we heard it all in snatched moments – in the fortnightly queue, on the radio news, in WhatsApp threads when data arrived – fleetingly, like a house martin.

Patterns, rhythms, the fabric of the everyday – we'd watched the threads that once tied our life together undo their coloured knots. This place to which we'd moved to seek our freedom, became the only place we'd ever been forced to stay. The 2 kilometres we were allowed to exercise in took us to the bog, only just, and I kept that walk for Sundays with the dog – alone. Both as ritual and as release. Sundays, in the dark, ancient bog, had become a form of ceremony, in an odd but soothing way.

That day the sun had hidden a little away; the golden light of the butterfly hours, just the day before, had shapeshifted; now it was a pale, metallic grey – like an insect, it glittered and glistened against shifting, wispy clouds. The dog, as always, had run ahead. I could hear her over the soft white cotton and the haunting, heart-aching snipe. Skylarks, too, were circling themselves back down towards the ground. Birch trees held us in our place. There was no wind of which to speak, all was still and shushed – not silent, of course, for there is no such thing as silence in such a living, breathing place. I smelled the gorse at all the edges of its folds, stroked the lichen on its scattered stone, walked through its teasel and thistle – the bog allowed the beat, the blood, the *me* of me, to crawl in close.

I knew – and this knowing, I see, has changed me – that this place existed, too, beneath my skin. I walked, and as I did I felt a loosening – as though the bog was creeping in beside the parts that make me up, the ones that keep me going. Beside the hard parts and the soft ones, the long ones and the short, I saw the creatures of us both begin to merge. And I know it makes me sound a little unusual, and I know I run the risk of being dismissed – but I feel I have no way to go than truly *with it*; with this feeling that has landed in my chest. Like the fledgling wren that flew, unbidden, through our front door, since first she came it's been so hard to coax her out. And so this feeling in my chest might never leave me, might hunker down like a finely boned, insistent baby bird. This sense that we are much less separate than we've been forced to believe. I knew it that day, walking through a bog so full of life and death. I knew that it and I existed in this same haunting, unknowable time – and that that meant something.

And then, in the middle of such thoughts, my dog was yelping. I heard the creatureliness of her body call me on. Ahead of me but many feet below me. She was struggling – in a V of water I had not even realised was there. Cut out from the space below us, a scar on the surface of the land. It formed a body of water; not a river in any 'natural' sense of the word, the water stagnant, black – peaty as the men that carved its lines. And there really was no moment where I actually, properly *thought*, no process kicked into gear through which I saw an ordered line. I was in and hauling her out before I knew it, and soon I realised it was a tighter V than it looked from up above. Up to my neck, in clothes now heavy with bog water, the V more narrow than I could have ever noted – no real room to even kick or move at all. And all around me the bog, with its living: keeping on. I tried to get a grip at the sides of the bank – swung as much as the limited space and energy would allow. A moment came when I felt my wellie sink and pull me down.

I've thought before of drowning, as outdoor swimmers often seem to do – but in my mind and in my dreams it was always deeper, darker – louder. I realised, at a point, that I would drown – if that was even what it would be called – with my head above this water. I would lose body temperature, I would lose consciousness, I would lose awareness, I would lose the thing inside me keeping the parts of me alive. It would be a simple thing, an ordinary, everyday event. I had put myself in this here body of water, and I would die here. It was so calm, it was so still. I gave up fighting it.

And I wish I could find a way to try to say it. I wish the words would find their way up from my guts. But I heard, above my head, the bog still living. I heard my dog, now free from the bog, sniff at the droppings by her feet. I heard, beneath my hair, the words of a local, as he handed me the first penknife I'd ever owned: 'Never hang about, girl, when ye think that you might need this. If it's in your head, it needs to get itself into your hands.'

It took five attempts to get my failing hands to clasp its silver into place. Then two or three to get its gleaming edge to grip – onto the only hanging root – high above my chest. I don't know how long I hung in place, or how long it took for me to haul my body up, far enough to catch the thick, hard bark of something growing at the top – just where I had entered.

The second I was safely spat out the dog set off, as though she had never stopped; running ahead, carrying on where she'd left off, going deeper into the body of the bog – keen to follow the scent of whatever living creature that she'd trailed. She didn't turn around, even once, until we'd left the bog behind us. Until she could no longer smell the creature that had called to her. Or until she felt the call back to her own home, louder than the smell.

The bruises on my body were like a night sky.
I stroked them as they blackened, then turned blue.

For weeks I was visited by birds of every colour.
I watched them as they flew into our home.

For weeks, I dreamed of every house I'd ever lived in.
For weeks, I dreamed of every place I'd ever left.

Saturday

A day, in the fourth month of the year's calendar, in the second season of the circle's turning, in the midst of the vastest, deepest unravelling we are told we've ever known.

See light that dances through hawthorn like a choreography of veins.

See dimpling & piercing, shimmering & flickering, see reflected & refracted – see a garden give itself over to glow & glimmer & gold.

Hear that day in the porcelain chamber of your ear.

Hear something that we always seem intent on calling silence.

Hear gentle weaving of wind through white may on the hawthorn.

Hear a small bird using the body of herself to make her nest.

Hear, in a part of the distance that you cannot see, a cuckoo – calling in such a way that you assume you are imagining it – conjuring its folkloric bones into being, on this echoey, searing afternoon.

Hear your own self, the parts of you both visible & not. Hear your aliveness as it courses through that time, & place, & more.

Smell it (this is the easy part): smell spring with all its green & white & yellow. Smell things beneath the ground in the fiercely delicate act of just becoming. Smell creaturely desire. Smell spring.

Taste it. Lift every smithereen of it with your hands, and lay it on your tongue. Swallow it down, into those places where you bring the outside in. Taste its salt & its silt, its sorrow & decay. Taste the day's blood like a mineral-rich beginning.

Touch – unseen, at first, unfelt. Firstly sensed in ways we have not learned to name.

Feel something land on warm, soft skin, on *your* warm, soft skin – feel something landing on the surface of your self.

Feel anticipatory stillness, feel flutter & beat. Feel the meeting
of another's being with your own.

Feel its feelers.
  Feel its feeling.
  Feel its feel.

Suppose a day, ordinary, normal. Suppose a Saturday in the
final week of April.
  Feel a butterfly land, for the very first time, upon your waiting
hand, quietly, with such fragile, aching grace.

Watch its powdery, exquisite wings, opening & closing,
  opening & closing, opening & closing.

See, without flinching – without stir of hand or arm –
  that it is injured.

Watch it dip in & out, in & out,
  of unseen, ghostly places.
  See the ebb and flow of it playing out
  upon the shoreline of your limb.

Suppose a day on which the earth is full
  of mourning, a toll of loss,
  that won't stop rising, like the sea.

Suppose a moment when we stood outside of time.
  When something came and held us firmly in our place.
  Suppose a day when there was time for standing still.
  A regular day, run-of-the-mill, flawless. The fiftieth day that
  you have stayed at home.
  Suppose that on this day a creature found your hand.
  Suppose a year where things unravelled like a pattern.

Like a marriage or a job, an economy or a rope,
suppose a year when life uncoiled like the mystery of DNA.

Suppose a time when we could choose to start again.

Suppose you cradle, on your hand, a speckled wood,
  feel its wing-beat in the hollow of your bones.
  Suppose you know – although you cringe to even share it –
that its tracing of your skin, it is a gift.

Suppose a spring quite unlike any you have ever known.
  Suppose a silken, solitary season, full of light & time & longing,
  hung like feathers, in a planet-bright sky.

Suppose a day where you might give yourself to being.
Suppose a day you might remember how to live.

Bealtaine, May

Milk Moon
Flower Moon
Planting Moon
Leaf Budding Moon
Egg Laying Moon
Moon When the Ponies Shed

Finch Child

I started dreaming about it less than a month after we first locked down. It came, at first, in April – the month I have long held the least affection for.

I say *it*, when to be perfectly honest – despite the fact the plumage does not easily give anything away in this variety of finch; the differences between the cock and hen as slight as the first vein of light on solstice – I knew *ab ovo* that *it* was a girl.

Not a female bird. No, it was not a hen finch at all. It was simply a *girl*. A very wee girl, at that. A girl-child of no more than three years of age, I would guess. She began to come to me in April 2020 – very early in that fourth month – just as the may began to come to the whitethorn, creamy, newly born. There had been so much whiteness in my world, that spring.

I had been, it must be told, rereading Han Kang's exquisite, fragmentary work *The White Book*, speaking out loud her list of white things like some incantation or keen.

I took, back then, to making my own list of that season's white things: a pink seed moon, the last frost, a collared-dove egg, the skull of a badger, blackthorn, the pelvic girdle of a rat, a pair of hidden cocoons, cabbage whites (in such un-imaginable abundance) and a season of waning grief.

> But *she* was not white, this finch child.
> She was golden & red & black & tawny.
> She was, this girl, a goldfinch child.

She was, this goldfinch child, a dream.
  She came that spring – the one like *no* other
  – the one like *every* other – in the dead of night.
  And when she came, she sang.
  I began to waken from dreams of things I'd never seen with
my own eyes but that felt like they could only have been taken
directly from my memory, so real and so fully lived was their
texture.
  Dreams of the northern lights above Shroove beach, green
& dancing, charged & primal – and it was her – that goldfinch
child – who had carried me there, somehow.
  Dreams of the River Foyle, meandering & inky black, then
stopped & frozen, with colossal whales singing up to us both
from beneath the ice – and her, tapping at the solid body of
water, as if to free them.
  Dreams of moths – delicately fashioned & finely painted,
graceful & prepossessing, weaving in and out of milking barns
& animal yards – flying through walls & gardens, above streams
& piles of rubble. The child sheltering them in her beak in
the moments when their strength visibly wavered.

*(And all the while this goldfinch girl, this colourful bird in a spring
of white things, filling the night's visions with her singing . . .)*

. . . and so what was there to do but try to unravel it all?

          . . . to try to find the way back to the beginning?

. . . to try to dig the story up at its very roots?

  But where might we start when it comes to imagined things?
Where is the foundation stone for invisible, insubstantial
                      objects?

Where was I supposed to look, to find the meaning – if any
– of this goldfinch child?

That particular spring – the one that mirrored its pair of
numbers like butterfly wings – continued, as well we all know
– and we found ourselves increasingly held in our places. Some
of us in places to which we may have only just arrived. Others
in places that we knew like the back of our own hands – places,
like our palms, that we had carried along with us, deep inside
our bodies, for all our lives. Some of us were kept in the one
place completely and utterly alone. Others were holed-up with
our whole family, with strangers, with folk with whom we
may never have shared more than a handful of words throughout
our entire cohabitation until that point. Some of us took to it
all like a skylark to the open blue, whilst others of us batted
against the restrictions – the unrecognisable world that daily
life had become – bashing our heads against the walls. We had
not, apparently, known we were living before these tectonic
shifts hit our plate. We had not, it has been said, ever really
realised how lucky we were to roam freely across the land, as
and when we so desired.

Of course some of us continued to roam, as freely as we felt
the sheer fact of our existence entitled us to. Some of us bent
the rules around themselves – twisted them & turned them &
blew them into the breeze – dandelion clocks. The numbers
rose & rose, like the sea, like a temperature, like the marks a
parent leaves behind in graphite on a white wall, traces of
the only visible form of growth their child made as the year
unravelled like a spool of red thread.

Loss, so much of it. Loss the like of which many of us had
never before even heard murmur of. It rippled through the
places we both knew and we did not. It soon ceased to be
about just places (if even it ever had been) and we realised that

the things that were at stake were not, in fact, *things* at all. Death, isolation, depression, uncertainty, poverty, fear and ache: this was the language of our loss. Humans, jobs, money, food, safety, touch and togetherness: this was its inventory.

It has changed us, this experience. It is changing us, still. We have no idea when it will end – *if* it will end – we are unsure what 'normal' might mean in the months and years to come. Since the very beginning, I could feel it moulding me, somehow. I could feel the pandemic's fingers tracing my skin and leaving their mark. The goldfinch child was really only the beginning, a tipping point in the midst of vast, unthinkable change. I would love to be able to veer clear of all cliché when it comes to the recollection of her visits (and of what I have taken her to represent). I found it hard, for quite some time, to speak of her. Try as I might, I could not loosen myself from her hold. Even when she left my nights, I found myself still woven into her feathers, the fabric of our beings intertwined. I'd waken from blank, emptied dreams – to light that really didn't quite belong – either to me, or to that place. Light that had no real right to be there, in that moment of such finely wrought and unsettling collective sorrow. Light that felt like it was suspended, not in the air but in an underlying space, a place – like memory – held beneath glass.

In time, I realised that she was, even in her absence, carrying something to me. Something I had left behind somewhere and had not, before this all happened, even realised I no longer had in my possession. It was unusual, you understand, every single ounce of it all. Her presence, her absence: *her*, quite simply. In the world outside – the world of mud & movement, birth & death, loss & hope – life continued, in ways that it both always had, and never had before this particular year.

This old stone railway cottage, the last dwelling before you reach the bog, gave itself over into the bright, soft hands of May. On the glorious first two days my lover and I sat in the garden we had spent weeks clearing, our hands red raw, our arms and legs still bearing the marks of our battle with the thorns and the brambles. This wilderness we had tamed with our limbs – for a wee while, at least. On the third day, just a few days before my lover's birthday, I awoke to a feeling I recognised but could not quite place. The sense of something either having shifted – having become somewhat dislodged – or perhaps having, in fact, been extracted from my insides entirely. How one might feel, say, when one wakens after surgery to find that cells, or a tooth, or an organ have been removed from the unseen parts of one's landscape. The light, still, was there but there was – in its bright whiteness – something that struck me as a little like a gap. A crack, a clearing, a perforation, a slit. There was a hole in the light that morning of the third day of May.

I went about my jobs, despite the disquietude the morning still held within its white-toothed, clenched jaw. Sorting of seeds in the shed, feeding of birds at the herb patch, drinking coffee in the burning sun, making notes in the shade of the sycamore tree, and then – out of nowhere – it came. The moment one might refer to (if one were so inclined) as the *cusp*. The sound muted – yet as clear as a moonlit night – of a creature making contact with glass. I looked up from the words in my hands (Oswald, I recall – always Oswald in the brightening month of May) and all of it came crashing down, every last shard of it. I could feel the smallest particles embed themselves in my salty, tingling skin. Not the window, of course; it remained firmly in its place. The thing that came down was the memory, you understand, the knowledge (in one fell swoop, like some injured tree) of what that dreamlike, disconcerting spring was really all about . . .

For there she was, just beneath my bedroom window
– that goldfinch child.
Her wee body all mangled.
Her wee eyes opening & closing against the brightness of
the changed world.

I cradled her in the nook of my jumper.

Held her as the beat of her body ebbed away.
The ethereal, fragile creature of her; gone.

1st

Copy-edits for TP.

No pilgrimage elsewhere. Our fire festival this year takes place in the places we each know the best: our own hearths, our own gardens, our own insides.

A bittern for the first time since Mull, a decade ago, as the smoke & ash worked their magic.

Stood beneath a circle of white and bawled as M tended the tall-flamed fire in silence.

What will the coming summer look like? And the winter?

Swallows, seeds and boom-boom-booming, beneath a Beltaine moon.

2nd

Such an incredible amount of butterflies in the lower field.

Worked in the garden (both types) as the dog slept in any shade she could find.

Watched Withered Hand on Insta Live as the sun set over Gorgie, and a bittern boomed over Correaly, and fuck are we *alive*.

And we must make each moment count.

3rd

Sat, for the whole joy-bright day, in the garden. Papers, coffee & goldfinches for my love's birthday. No visitors to the laneway but the cuckoo and a butchering ginger tabby. Feared, again and again, for the wrens. Cried at kind message from G on Instagram, as sun set − peach streaks against faded gold. It all feels too much, the goodness that still lives in the world, despite it all.

IM picked a card from the deck for me, L sent me it in the afternoon's bright sun: PLANTING SEEDS. I can't even process how it made me feel; how much I want to grow something inside of me, how it won't let me go.

4th
Sat outside looking at so much growth in the seedlings, as a cuckoo calls & calls & calls.

5th
Brought in, for the table, blackberry leaves and cow parsley. Placed them in the sage-green enamel milk churn. Seeing it against the yellow Formica made me feel like me again for the first time in so long. Is this ridiculous? Am I ridiculous? Do I care?
The moon above the trees, in that pale electric blue only to be found here, was somewhat shocking. How can it all be real: the moon, the sky, the moon in the sky? The moon in the sky, and us still here beneath it? Is it possible to fall in love with a field? With white blossom blowing in a gentle breeze? With the light that touches both, making untameable things of them?

So close to finishing TP that I could weep. The hawthorn, in the early evening, seemed to urge me onwards, seemed to say it will all be OK. When the book is done, I am cutting off all my hair and giving it to this wild, beautiful garden.

6th
Already the blue tits are taking my hair for their nests, just minutes after I cut it all off.

7th
Nigella and nasturtium seedlings, pushing up to meet the morning sun.
White cuckoo flower in the top field, tall but tender.
Cleavers in the bottom field.
Is it possible to fall in love with a spider?

8th

Lilac, flowering nettle and one I cannot name. I am trying to find a way to remain grounded, and these fields full of flowers feel as good a way as any.

Chard seedlings are up.

M planted the strawberry J gave us, just to the left of the sycamore.

I planted the first row of lettuce into the container made from leftover decking.

Watched, from the sofa M made from a Victorian metal bed, the silently setting sun.

Red and orange, then lilac and purple, then gone.

9th

Reread, in the early light, the piece I wrote for Máthair last year on motherhood.

Unsure why I was so shocked that I cried. Why I felt so ashamed to. Why I apologised to M as though he would not understand (how could he not?).

I am such a fucking mess.

Coffee in the sun as we sort our seedlings.

Moved both hydrangea bushes to the laneway in the hope they thrive there.

The great tits took, after I had brushed her, the dog's hair with which to build.

I felt giddy with excitement at it, unable to contain my joy.

We ate, with pasta at lunch in the sun, the first things we have grown: cress & rocket, all topped with edible flowers. The giddiness continues.

With dinner: micro broccoli, micro red Russian kale, micro rocket, wild vetch, dandelion and herb robert. Find this all, as well as clichéd, exceptionally electrifying.

10th
More yellow in the garden that I have ever seen. Rereading *The Grassling*, of course.
We have decided, against every odd, to try for a baby.

11th
Moths, moths, so many moths.

Reminding me that there is beauty in this world the like of which I could never have dreamed. Before this time, I used to say I'd attend to the moths once I'd done all my work. They came & they came & they came. Then I said I'd do the work once the moths stopped coming. Now I wonder if the moths *are* the work.
I have begun to paint again. Just colour and shape, like on our Steiner teacher training, and my oh my is it helping. So grateful to have hands. Rereading *Handiwork*.

Making a list of white things:

> M's gift of bog cotton (a fortnight after I fell into its
> deep, black waters)
> bones
> eggs
> hawthorn
> the first whitethroat
> fallen flowers from the strawberry plant
> the pebbles I gathered in the Burren
> all the cabbage whites (so many of them)
> the ghost swifts in the lower field at dusk; like lights
> above a harbour, almost.

Sat listening to John Kelly whilst the email came through to say copy-edits are complete on TP.

He was playing the Blue Nile, and my favourite of theirs at that. The may is out, the wren is building in the sycamore. The blue tits in the eaves, and I am so so grateful for this life, come what may.

Rereading Mark Roper's work. Reminded of his words I have copied in the front of my journal: 'We are held by what cannot be held.'

12th

It is so bright, it is so bright, it is oh so so so bright.

Candles (dripping their beautiful colours over this once-white holder by my bed).

Veins of it on top of clover in the big field.

Strings of it in the cow field at the close of day as grey clouds fill the midnight-blue body of the sky.

Drops of it on dried seed-heads at the barn; golden & silent.

13th

Seamair, so soft and purple and full of hope.

Clover, oh clover, and wild wild strawberry.

Violet, and (possibly) pignut.

Awake, last night, until way after four. Worst night since this began. Years of worry and sorrow flooding back over me that I thought had long been got rid of. Thinking of many, so many, who will find this so triggering. The uncertainty. The darkness. The lack of family support. The not-feeling-safe-again of it all. Spent the morning beside a single pink foxglove and felt unthinkably glad for my lot. Overwhelmingly grateful.

It seems the light has fallen for the cow parsley.

14th
Aloneness.
Openness.
Gratefulness.

TP arrived with A on her birthday, which fills me right up, full to the top with it all, with all the feelings I could even claim to know.

A damselfly, keeping me company, for almost a full hour.
  Lightness.

15th
Stood, as the evening made to close, beneath the wren's nest in the sycamore tree, sending out love to every woman keeping a safe nest through these times, for themselves, for others if there are any, for the child inside of them, too.
The wren is unfazed when I am near. It feels the most inimitable gift of all, her trust.
K's seeds are up – green and full and dancing.
M made for me, as I baked the bread, the cleverest frame for the broad beans. He is some man for one man, as they say.

16th
As I read a deeply moving piece by Laura Barton about trying to have a baby, something so delicately woven with my own insides too, M returned from the laneway with possibly the most gorgeous nest I have ever set eyes on. It took this gift, somehow, to let it all set in, how harrowing these last months have been. Editing a book, my first one – one that begins to touch the surface of my relationship with home, not mothering, abandonment and more – all done at the end of a laneway, during a global pandemic. Laura's gorgeous, raw words felt such

a gift, too; like the nest, a way to feel again. A way to feel, for feeling is what I need, what we all do, perhaps. The nest is the second he has found for me during this time. I have also found two, one I sent to J and wrote a little about. There are two more in the eaves of our small home. Another in a fallen ash branch at the foot of the garden.

There is such meaning in what finds us, and when it does.

In the top field: peacock butterflies in the making, and a single female orange tip.

Rebecca May Johnson's piece for *Granta* this week on her allotment was such soothing balm.

Placed, into the earth in our first garden, the roses we bought in the Bogside, back when I felt broken beyond fixing.

Holding, being held, letting go, healing.

The gift of the soil.

All around the garden under this morning's poised crescent moon, frilly green poppies are showing their bodies to the world. Some are Californian, and I think they will be of peachy, orange hues. Some are from C in Sligo, and I have no idea what they'll be like. I hope they come strong and well; I am so excited to see their delicate, dancing heads. I wonder if they will be able to be dried out, kept to send to friends and placed around our home. The roses are budding, too, and I wonder what colour the foxgloves will be. The joy this garden brings me is almost too much, sometimes; often, in fact.

At dusk, a buff ermine on the window outside my desk. Soft, haunting; almost dead.

17th

Roses, though, what a thing.

So many caterpillars in the bog, and another (or the same) buff ermine when I arrived back − thought dead − alive, though.

Day 70 at home.

(Creamy white / Ochre / Bark Brown
Gifts / Delicacy / Strength
Things thought dead that are alive / Things in their place /
Things in their becoming.)

Field notes, with Kathryn Joseph on repeat: '*How do I let go of all this fucken love?*'

18th

M has replaced the broken head on his lovely modified Hadrill & Horstmann wooden lamp. He took the broken shade off the ceiling in our bedroom too, and replaced it with a buttercup-yellow one off an old Herbert Terry Anglepoise. Now the yellow flex is so bright and striking – just the right size now too. He is such a good fixer of broken things.

I managed to buy seeds, and all feels as though it could be OK, somehow.
Dragonflies in the strong sun, as I gathered wild mint from the stream's edge.
A full and reassuring day's work in the garden. I am so grateful for this space, this place, much more than I could ever put into words.
Sowed the Opal Creek peas directly, so encouraging was the midday sun.
Anne Carson's words as I make for almost-summer sleep: 'Brilliant deaths cut / the day . . . even the lark does not see the Open, someone / said in another time.' I am back in it all again, the ache and the unquantifiable nature of it all.

19th

Woke feeling low. Returned from the grey fields to find M had dubbined my boots and I bawled with love for him, with gratitude.

When I posted the image of the moth from Sunday that we assumed was dead but was alive, C said: 'It's mad how they find you.' K: 'Did it let you snuggle?' This morning I drew a moth that was not that moth, the wing of the one I drew was too undamaged, it was too small and had far less spots. The one I drew was one that I woke up to find on my pillow in the blinding light of the morning. Perhaps another buff, or maybe a white ermine, but either way I cannot quite believe I slept the night – all of it, perhaps – with a moth within inches of me. It feels, as it always does, like a gift from an unknown place.

Received, in the post, from an unknown giver, *Bird By Bird* by Anne Lamott. Utterly impeccable timing. Sowed, after devouring it in one sitting, what I hope will become bright yellow Craspedia in honour of S who I miss so ridiculously much. M made raised beds from old telegraph poles. Working on the herb garden just now, hands mucky and glad; so mucky and so glad. Found a may beetle, such an odd creature. Such a hard, weird day but everything is going to be OK.

20th
18 months sober this week. What a thing. What a time.
Sowed, directly into the earth, scabious and quaking grass.

21st
Awoke in the softness of morning to the sense that something was in the house. Went into the living room to find a speckled fledgling flying around the room. Managed to open the window to let the delicate, new bird back out into the world.
Reread, for the umpteenth time, Kathleen Jamie's 'A Lone Enraptured Male' essay and was drawn, as if reading them for the first time, to these words: 'To give birth is to be in a wild place.'

The day began with a speckled bird and ended with a speckled moth.

22nd
So stormy.
Woke to find the whole greenhouse collapsed, carried across the garden by the night's winds.
I think I've lost them all.
I feel broken, so broken.

23rd
Spent six silent hours making L a birthday poem from found words. About the bird-child from my dream. I have no idea how or why but it shifted something so huge inside me; for which I am exceptionally grateful. Withered Hand on for the whole day. We never could have known how much some people meant to us before now. It's been a fucking hard ride but it feels like it might be just about to get a little bit lighter.
A year and a half sober. Just now, as the day began to quieten down, as the sun made its way behind the tall trees, I had one of the most important conversations of my life.
Stop silencing her, that bird singing in your soul.
Keep these words as a reminder, ever and always, stop fucking with your own desire.

24th
Playing in the dancing light, dreaming in the shadows.
A year and a half sober, which feels the biggest deal of my life so far. Not allowed to swim so celebrated by walking the same fields as we have every day for months; each step taken a means of giving thanks – for the grace that got me through.
A female chaffinch, still warm, on the laneway. There is always a dead bird, on days such as these.

Cow parsley in such unimaginable abundance, and I love it this year; much more than ever before.

Stood halfway up the top lane for almost an hour just watching it dance in the soft breeze; observing the shadow it made of its own self. It felt, in ways I did not understand, like the most important thing I could be called on to do in these days.

Fennel, the smell of it, the look of it, the yellow of it.

Fennel in the yellow month of May.

25th

The first foxglove has opened, only just, at the bottom. It is pale lilac/pink – like dawn or a Mediterranean dusk. Tiny darker specks on its inners, like the wee fledgling.

26th

Spent the whole morning looking at the collection of stones between the two flower beds; gathered from almost every corner of this island. The middle part – two grey-white Burren stones on top of a wooden structure, fixed to concrete M found further up the line – reminds me of Barbara Hepworth. I love how the light falls on it. A simple, gorgeous thing. All at once I am flooded by the fear that I might never swim in Cornwall again and must catch myself on. As if that matters at all with what is really going on right now. Sometimes my selfishness leaves me queasy.

27th

Rereading Rebecca Solnit's *A Field Guide to Getting Lost*. My oh my she is so incredible: 'Sometimes gaining and losing are more intimately related than we like to think.'

Back again, this week, with Kathleen Jamie. Her essay for Little Toller on Brexit – the best closing words of any essay in existence: '(I still love the world.)' YES YES YES YES YES.

A setting pink sun on the eightieth day at home, and I am ready for bed, bone-tired and full of hunger.

28th

G tagged me in a post on Instagram, a memory from two years back of when she held – in her smooth, ringed hand – a moth. Yesterday she had held – in the same hand – a heart-shaped stone. These poetic coincidences feel like the self's reminder of its bones: delicate and white
(like snow like gaps like suffering like anger like beauty like ghosts) . . .

29th

First rose of summer, and of our new home.
Yesterday M took down all the wooden barricades from the house's front door. When I walked out of it this morning, for the very first time, the rose had – I imagine – only just opened up, creamy, stroked pink.
Read, with tears in my eyes and shame the whole way through my body, Ross Gay's poem about Eric Garner, who 'put gently into the earth / some plants which . . . / continue to grow . . . / making it easier for us to breathe.'
A black man was murdered by those we are told are meant to protect us.
What the fuck is this world, even?

31st

Another ermine, playing on my hand, as I secured the creamy-lilac clematis to the wall.

An Unlit Stove

This is how it happened, the preposterous shift in the landscape of the everyday, to make room in our conversations for *baby*.

It happened like a landslide.

It happened slowly, incrementally, in ways that added up over the years but that could not be noticed, let alone measured, in any given moment along the way.

It happened the way the ending of any given day does, I suppose.

It had happened, already – long before I made to unlock my phone to capture it; to Instagram it; to try to mark its happening in any real or solid way.

It happened all out of nowhere (although we both knew – as you likely do, too, that that statement was a million miles from being true).

Once, in the very early days of my relationship with M, my father offered me a solitary piece of advice; the only words of guidance he had offered me since I was a small child. He told me that, when an argument occurred, the only thing to do, whatever the weather, was to go outside. To put a stop to all that was happening indoors – leave the plates on the table, turn out the lights, gather coats and whatever else might be needed – and get outside. Get up off the floor, the bed, the chair, the edge of the bath – and walk together – side by side. Change the scenery, the tempo, the flow of a given moment and you change everything in that moment irrevocably. You cannot, he told me, drag yourself back into a full-blown barney when you find yourself outside under the sky, under any sky that's there for the having.

I cannot speak of the changes that occurred for my lover – the ones that made him decide, one glorious May evening – dog walked, dinner prepared – to leave the stove unlit. To alter the course of our normal evenings just enough as to unsettle us into the path not widely taken. There was no barney blowing up. There was not, neither had there been for as long as either of us could remember, an argument on the horizon. The day *babies* entered our conversations, our home, our relationship, was not quite warm enough to leave the stove unlit in our small stone cottage.

The day it all really happened – that unimaginable unsettling – much like the month in which it fell, had been gorgeous. Gorgeous in that way of simple, uncluttered things. M did not need to take us outdoors for there was no argument to try to halt. We had, in fact, only just gone *inside*, after another day spent tending to our newly cleared garden. There was very little else for any one of us to be doing that month. No, by choosing not to light the stove, by choosing to sit down, take my hands in his, and leave the busyness of the evening for another time, he unsettled the flow of the everyday – just enough to change every single thing in existence. Instead of clearing away the day before's ashes, taking them outside, chopping large pieces of wood into smaller ones for kindling; instead of coming back inside carrying these offerings in his hands; instead of criss-crossing them in the grate, instead of placing small bits of leftover coloured candle wax in between to get the fire started (a stove rainbow), instead of allowing himself to be carried along in the gentle but firm flow of the routine of everyday lives; their orderly ritual – he stepped *outside* of every last bit of it.

In truth this loosening, this blurring, this opening, this tear in the backcloth of our reality – the one that allowed us, somehow, to break many years of silence about *babybabybaby* – happened as simply as the way a day unfolds. That is purely to say there was no point at which we opened any door and let the changes to our lives enter in. There was, simply, a man who decided not to light the stove, a handful of months into a global pandemic. A man who, realising that life might never be the way it once had been before – who, understanding that the everyday was far from everyday any longer – decided to pull a little at the tear that he could already see.

It didn't really happen because the stove remained unlit.
It *did* really happen because the stove remained unlit.
It happened because we (he) simply *broke the silence*.

For, you see, as P. Ögn said, quite some time before this one, 'Silence is two things
though only one: a thrush on the heath, a wizen bone.'

We had never, not even once, in the whole seven years of loving one another, talked of *babies*.
They had, of course, come along at various twists and turns along our shared path.
People close to us made babies and we shared our lives with them as closely as we could.
People close to me made babies and thought it would be a wondrous thing if I (despite a plethora of odds stacked against me) made them too.
People close to me made babies and (thinking it would be a wondrous thing if I made them too) told me so.
People close to M made babies – or didn't make them and (thinking it would be a ridiculous thing if he made them) told him so.
Babies were everywhere, all the time – as always they are – but still we never spoke of them, not even once. Not when each year crept around the corner, reminding us that time is an oddly boned creature; one that waits – as well you know – for no woman.
Never once did we sit together and talk about the delicate nuances that marked our lives. Things that made it seem certain

that babies were definitely not a thing on our horizon. Things such as illness, age, circumstance, money, the past, the future, the present.

Never once did we talk about babies.

Neither could I say there was silence, even though neither of us ever said a word about them until that day.

(It happened *because it happened*, of course, as is the way with every single thing that ever comes to pass.)

Meitheamh, June

Blooming Moon
Strawberry Moon
Rose Moon
Hot Moon
Mead Moon
Berries Ripen Moon
Green Corn Moon
Honey Moon
Hatching Moon
Birth Moon

Particular years,
like particular places
(like particular creatures)
show us that
even an absence
can cast such beautiful
shadows;
in a particular
vein of light.

Púca

A white form dancing against cold blue tiles, red liquid drop-
ping in a bleach-white bowl (again). I'm still not sure which
thing unsettled me the most on that echoey grey morning, at
the swiftly falling end of June. Out to the small kitchen,
Mooncup in hand, to boil the kettle, and it follows me. We are
a two, now, in the wee space kept for cooking and for cleaning,
for sterilising – not bottles for the feeding of young, but a
vessel for the collection of blood: *my* blood, red & constant; a
primal language. It, this other thing, bats against the window
but will not leave when I open it up. The kettle has boiled, so
I fill the pan and light the hob – and as the vessel bobs on its
bubbling sea, I think of the moon that it has been named for
– how this creature reminds me of it; grey flecks on its tissue
wings, like craters, like parts where water must once have traced
the surface, silently.

*(The day I knew you weren't coming, nothing took the colour or the
shape it was supposed to.)*

The day you were a thing less real than even the unreal sea,
less real than even the unreal years, I wept like a baby on the
filthy, freezing bathroom floor.

The day I knew you were not you, I finally breathed out.

I finally accepted that I was – in choosing to properly grieve
for you – learning to feel again.

I had been reading (trying to read) a book L sent me about
light, but it was hurting my heart too much, leaving me fraught
and weary. Instead of feeling hopeful – about returning to the
places of which it spoke – I felt even more despondent. The
rain would not stop. The laneway would not lengthen.
The days would not change. I began to see myself there, on
that wet laneway – for ever. I saw a life unfurl that did not at

all resemble the life for which I had been striving; for which we both had. I did not wish, any longer, to read, to think, to write about light. I simply wished to experience it. I wanted to be in the light. To lay my tired body inside its glow. To know radiance in my days. To trust that it might stay. Truth be told, I had already understood it was not really about light. Truth be told when I thought of light, these days, I thought of you. And when I thought of you, these days, I was too full of yearning to even think straight. The longing had grown limbs, was taking over the insides of me.

The creature, still, is tracing a pathway across my small stone home.

This way and that, stopping – briefly – only to take, once more, to the indoor air.

Back into the bathroom in which we met, then out again, never stopping, never letting itself rest, even for the briefest of moments.

I want to name this space in which I've found myself – to call this bordering time something very particular – a specific kind of marginal, gossamer 'place', but I resist. I am done with such liminality, you see.

This time of trying & willing & hoping (& all that) leaves me tired – in the way of dashed hopes & endings of things that I had assumed would last for ever. Only a handful of days in, and already I feel defeated which is ridiculous. Of course you are not coming yet. We have only just begun to speak of you (oh how it feels to speak of you), to try for you; to make space for you. Of course you are not coming yet (how could you be coming yet?). And yet I feel broken by these drops of blood which mean, of course, that you are not coming yet. To think at all about the fact that I know in my heart of hearts that you are likely never coming is too much just now. You are not coming *yet*, but there will be days in many of the months ahead where there will be, once more, the chance that you are coming. To even have that glimmer, the small but perfectly formed hope that you could, in fact, be coming, is more than I ever dreamed of.

The creature will not sit at peace.

Colliding with the Connemara stone on the dusty window ledge, it calls me as if by name.

Calling my eye from the stove to the field, calling me – even as it remains inside – out to the outside world. At first, I do not listen. I allow myself the time to grieve.

I am not, of course, grieving for you.

I am, of course, grieving for you.

I am not, of course, brokenhearted.

I am, of course, brokenhearted.

For all of the time spent pretending I was OK.

All of the tears and frustration, for all of the *poor wee me*.

I am trying to work through emotions that I cannot even name.

The feelings that, even more than a decade down the line, still feel alien.

I am trying to honour the way I feel right now, as well as the way I felt back then – the way I felt in all of the *back thens*. A decade and a half of making peace with not being a mother, then a month and a half of making peace with trying – against all the odds – to be a mother. Somehow the time periods are comparable. Somehow the time periods are non-existent. Somehow, I have to push away the what ifs: if we'd talked sooner, decided sooner, tried sooner. Somehow, I have to trust the process. Believe that what is right will find a way, accept that I am happy as I am (*we* are happy as we are) and believe that everything will be OK no matter what.

Somehow, I have to be OK.

Out it goes, at last, to the day that is making way for the gloaming.

I watch it for as long as I can manage, then lose it in a blur of branch and meadow.

> The meadow in the gloaming, then.

The grass tall and full of summer creatures like that first one – lekking – dancing with such abandon. Dionysian, charming, brilliant.

> I stay with them
> for longer
> than I really understand why,
> then return inside
> – cramps making their way
> across my belly and my back
> – ready for whatever may come.

1st

Observation, the act of really looking and listening, attending to the world around us, feels so necessary.

Black Lives Matter movement & campaigns to protect abuse victims in media to extent never have witnessed before. The time to listen & act is now.

2nd

Sat in the bright, first light with Richelle Kota's work this morning.

5th

ALL MOTHERS WERE SUMMONED WHEN HE CALLED OUT FOR HIS – graffiti shared over and over today on Instagram. It is too much to even try to contemplate but we must.

6th

Landworkers' Alliance statement on the link between racism and food has made me so keen to learn. Tending to any stretch of land is part of the history of violence, and I need to know I am not going at it blindly.

7th

A photo of a heavily pregnant Black woman holding a sign:

WE ARE NOT CARRYING FOR NINE MONTHS
THEN STRUGGLING DURING LABOR FOR NINE HOURS
JUST FOR YOU TO KNEEL ON THEIR NECK FOR NINE
MINUTES

and fuck am I broken. Have no idea where to begin (what white privilege to even feel that way; not to have to fight it every second of every day, what a fucking mess).

Tonight I picked things I grew from seed, the evening the world took steps towards a future based on equality.

Clover, snapdragon, fuchsia, nasturtium, pansies, lettuce, rocket, purple basil: a rainbow of solidarity; a meal of hope.

Read M June Jordan's 'Calling on All Silent Minorities' before bed; 'WE NEED TO HAVE THIS MEETING / AT THIS TREE / AIN' EVEN BEEN / PLANTED / YET'.

L shared earlier that silence is violence and I agree. We need to call this shit out. I am struggling to find the words and in fact I don't think they are mine to find, they are mine for the listening; we need to learn to listen, finally.
Lucille Clifton, Lucille Clifton, Lucille Clifton. 'Let the men keep tender / through the time . . .' Black men are teaching their babies how to show police the sign of peace and I am livid. How did we get here? How do we get out?

8th
They come to me, always, as the turning world changes beyond all recognition. Today was, of course, the day for a fox to find me as I walked the dog in the top field as the sun began to set. This beautiful, hopeful, flaming, turning world.

9th
I dreamed last night no baby came. I was old and M was gone. I was alone, more alone than I thought a person ever could be, and I woke up shivering.
Gathered from the garden, in the early morning, roses. The peach and the pink of them against the bright, mauve-streaked sky might stay with me always. The cosmos are out, all purple and full of movement, beneath the first foxglove. The scabious, too. Dirt beneath my nails and light on the old sleepers and I am grateful, oh so grateful.

10th
Teilgean: cast, throw
Solas: light
How is it that sometimes when we cast away, or throw something off, veins of illuminating light ripple through the harbour. Moved beyond measure by Nick Hand's words on Bristol tearing down that statue.

Claire Ratinon's poster:

BLACK LIVES MATTER

FUCK YOUR FUCKING FRENCH BEANS

sums up the despair many of us felt watching gardening accounts we love pretend nothing had happened last week. Yes to reflective silence but no to taking up instead of making space. We need to do so much better.
There is much pain in this world but much beauty too. It is up to us to be the carvers of hope.
Stood, in the meadow as tall grasses and countless flowers danced and wept.
White woman's tears are not enough.

11th
Woke, for the second time, to a bird in the house. This morning – a house martin. There now are five sets of birds – nesting or fledged – within a handful of feet of the front door.
What does it mean to notice and to record such things in one's day?
What are they trying to tell me? Am I listening? (Oh my, am I listening.)
Alice Vincent's words on gardening today moved me in their raw simplicity: 'Gardening is beautiful, gardening is meditative, gardening

can be gentle. But to deny its politics is to deny its power.'

Received in the post, right after we ran out, a delivery of homemade granola from L. Unsure why this felt so utterly and incredibly affecting.

I broke the trowel.

Heavy rain took, off the most delicious, large white Californian poppy, all the petals; revealing the gorgeous velvet purple inners. Strawberry and lavender in the returned light, but no flowers yet on the nasturtium by the sycamore.

Gathered sage, rosemary and thyme, which all felt so important; so fitting, in an odd and inexplicable way. And garlic scapes, to have in the pizza sauce. The broad beans have started to flower.

12th

Still a no for the broadband here. So much work lost these last months, and now no way to take on the wee bits I'm being offered, but I grew a rainbow and held it in my mucky hands, and that makes it feel OK, for now.

13th

Have been wakening to birds in the house, fledglings in the soft pink hush of morning, beating against my bones: wanting to be let back out into the bright, still world.

So many unseen birds & bees today, so many unquiet voices. And seen bees, too, so many on the lavender, in the foxgloves, both.

Life is now divided into then & now.

Reading Alice Oswald before – never having tended to a garden – and reading Alice Oswald now – as if for the very first time. The pak choi bolted.

15th
'Let there be new flowering / in the fields.' Lucille Clifton.
I feel like a new world is on its way, winging its way towards
our hearts. We are being offered the chance to sculpt it, to be
part of the new story. This world is not a safe one until all of
us feel safe. I am trying to find balance in these new fields.
There is much grief, much sorrow, much loss – but there is
much promise, too.

16th
What even is time?

17th
Found Jessica J. Lee writing about learning to make soy sauce
so beautiful, heart-wrenchingly so. 'In the past sixteen years, I
have moved house more times than I can count . . . I am
reaching my mid-thirties, and I simply want time and space.
As much as I want a child . . . I want to learn to make soy
sauce.'
Yes, simply, time and space.

18th
Breacóg, small magpie moth, as I made for bed last night.
2 days with another, furry, pale-yellow moth by my desk. 102
days in this wee stone cottage. It feels surreal to imagine ever
seeing the sea again but in eleven days I'll see the Atlantic for
the first time since winter.

19th
Nearing the end of a funny old week. Every single thing I try
to write ends up fiction instead of non. The words are surreal,
fucked up and so different from before. I'm different, too, so
I suppose it makes sense. Seem unable to write the old stuff
in the old way any more.

Moths & bones & nests & newts & time; like an old swan, stripped bare.

Been thinking about how tired you would be if you'd been fighting for your right to your life since the day you were born. It is not enough just to say we are not racist. We must be anti-racist. It is the only way through this horror we have taken as normal.

The day ends with pink candles, chamomile tea and a huge pearlescent poppy.

If joy is to be found in the way we live each day, then surely this is it, the noticing and the holding close, the honouring and the loving.

20th
  moths
  moths
  moths
  moths

(hiding inside the bones)
                        Moths everywhere and always.

Today: on the first *Winter Pages* – ghost-white against sky-blue, on Sarah Gillespie's *Moth* book.

22.43, the Solstice.

First one not in the sea since moving back to Ireland. A week of deep disappointment, culminating in pissing rain today, and breaking the candle-holder LT sent me, which left me howling crying. She has been like a mother when I have needed it most. Left me really considering objects, once more; their pull so like a wave.

'True Hope Cometh from the Sea' – a story in the *Moth*

magazine – has buoyed me – simply through its title. Soon, we all will see her again, soon. Those of us who miss her in ways we can never quite explain.

My love called me over to the coffee table, right where I smashed the holder, to show me that, when he looked, instead of the broken part there was, on the floor, a small white feather. These things, if we let them, really come. The light may be bleeding out but what grace it leaves beside our bones.

21st

Trending, on Twitter, in Ireland once more: #Ibelieveher. When the fuck will we ever learn to keep our women safe?

New moon / solstice / naked swim in glacial lake.
Rosemary, kept near to me, unsure why.
Pulled the radishes and gathered more edible flowers than my hands could carry.
Need a basket.

Sara Baume's commission for Cork Midsummer Festival is achingly good.
In red and in lower case: 'so sick and tired of parsimony, we long for debauchery'.

22nd

(always light)
It is the turning of the year, the still point of the summer solstice has passed. We are making our way towards the next part of the circle. Middling, gossamer time. The light out there is fading. I watch it bleed out from a new moon, solstice sky. Particular light, though, when it comes, it comes to change us. Some light, when it comes, it comes to stay.
Ghost swift, all yellow, all velvet, all dance – in my open hands.

23rd

12.44 a.m. − a *mothery* (the only word for it) at our yellow front door, of course.

Later, the most beautiful, heavy, charcoal pebble from C, sent from Scotland.

Objects like these mean so much more these days, more than I even know how to understand.

St John's Eve.

Painted, full of sadness in the afternoon light, the clover in the top field. Purple and white.

Storm-strong, gossamer-light.

Fire laid, then a swim in the top lough, to mind me through the year.

We are changed, all of us I think, by this time held in one place.

I don't know where I am any more.

I search in the early hours of dawn but I've forgotten what I'm looking for; who.

Tonight, the veil is at its thinnest, and I am ready.

Some things are not lost, never could be I hope.

The bones are ready for offering.

Moths, three of them, with snouts.

24th

Always, on St John's, I seem to find myself fixated on time. On what it even is.

This year I do not think I can even try to go there. I am so shook by it all.

Yellow butterflies, in the yellow of morning.

The lavender is divine, just now, such a gift.

The rain has made a pond of the carved oak bowl.

The lady's mantle is growing, at last. At least some good came of all the rain.

Sea thistle. Wish I knew more about its history, a pre-colonial existence, but here I fall short, again.

25th
Audre Lorde, again. 'The quality of light by which we scrutinize our lives has direct bearing upon the product which we live, and upon the changes which we hope to bring about through those lives.'
Louder.
New dongle held out for the whole of the Alice Oswald lecture. Sat, with coffee, on the front doorstep and nearly wept with gratitude.

26th
Trace arrived. Feel certain it will affect me deeply.
Derravaragh.
Swam beneath a cormorant, a curlew, mating dragonflies, swallows, swifts and teenagers.
Storm sky.
Heron on the shore.
Lake formed from the cycles of ice.
Tears as consolation for death / water as surface and not / grief as stopped & unstopped
Then, before bed, a light emerald.
The green of it, the dance of it, the enchantment.
Lorde again, her words on the erotic as power. How we grow to know ourselves, what to do when we forget.

27th
At the front door in the dark, the moths fly around me like a dreamscape, and I am haunted by it. This summer will leave, for ever, the residue of their wings, the sound of our coexistence on this small stretch of dark land.

Why they came. Why the moths came.
Lauret Savoy's unequivocal words on the pre-existence of the
world as conversation between stones, as the storm rages outside,
and I am finally still.

28th
Unending winter.
I need to mark this season, this unending time, in which way
I am not yet sure.
Red skies at night-time. Traces of something in the clouds,
something I can't grasp.
Tried to paint it – made the gaps into gold dots.
What we hold of the land as a trace; what it holds of us.

Tomorrow we can leave Westmeath for the first time since
March. Those of us who stuck to it in Ireland have been
county-locked for a third of a year. Those of us in this county
– here in the middle – have been farthest from the sea that
we could ever be on the island. We are islanders. It is completely
against our make-up to be away from the sea for so long. I
am happy to have followed advice, glad to keep others safe but
so fucken ready to see the sea. Oh my own privilege, my own
bullshit, etc.

29th
Brain has been like a boggy quagmire for a month now. Need
to stop guilting myself about what I haven't managed to do
these last months. We are living through something we have
no experience of, no control over. We can only try, we can
only do our best.
'This is a great moment in the life of humanity and it is
rich with the possibilities for change.' Ben Okri, for ever and
always.

Sharmaine Lovegrove posted about those doing 'the work',
asking if people really are ready; awake and prepared to
change things. Her last sentence speaks volumes; 'This. Ends.
Now.'
Got back in the Atlantic Ocean and honestly I can't find the
words, I don't even want to.
Me in the sea, the sea in me. And I realise this is how it was
the whole time, how it has always been, always will be.
Wild, grey & unknown.
Bought, for the first time in months, candles. Seems such a
small thing to bring such joy.
In Bell, Book & Candles, found, beside the children's books, a
copy of Didion's *The Year of Magical Thinking*. The time is here
to read it, it seems.
Lunch in Kai. Oh me oh my.
Spent March, April, May and June at home. Most weeks I
thought at least once of a particular drainpipe in Galway, in
the Westend – all rust and various sea-foam greens. Went, as if
on pilgrimage, to visit it today, and my heart was glad.

30th
(The pages of my first book arrived for me to check.)

Grateful & joyful & lightlightlight; there is so much light.

Halfway through this year of winged creatures.

Moths, in numbers unlike anything we had ever seen before.
Birds, so many soft, close birds.
Birds, so many birds, and so close that we could, and did,
hold them in our hands.

In April and May, in the light like none before it, in a turning,
emptied world, we had watched as our home, quietly, became
theirs. My love cut, in the highest gold one noon, the straggled
hairs of me and the dog, and watched them scatter, clumps of
brown and fawny cream, beside the seedlings I still can't believe
we grew. Cornflowers and lettuce, foxgloves and beans. Hair
in every corner, we watched in disbelief as birds swooped down
to claim it for their own. Great tits in the eaves, blue tits in
the gap the rats had made above the dripping gutter; their
fluttering, awkward movements above our heads, in bed, as we
held each other close in stroking heat. The wrens played it safe,
two nests in place of one, and how we worried when the
sycamore tree grew hushed. The cat, in wont of butchering,
revealed the second nest. We chased him from our fledglings
like a crow. The farmer only believed the house martins when
she saw them. They have, says she, not come this way in decades.
The door had just been painted when they came, 'crushed
lemon', now speckled brown with dripping mud, like a song
thrush.

And I know, it seems, that this could never happen, but I
have learned, it seems, to forget about being believed. And so
this is how it happened, then, at sunrise, on the first summer
solstice that we've spent in this new world —

The door has been left open through the night. I awaken, as
if called by my full name, as if called out to the living room,
by the presence of another, called to the blood and bone, the
heat and beat, the flutter and the fear. The dog, in the corner,

wakens too, and we are a three now in this room, and one of us wants out. One of us is scared, and wants back out, to the world in which she has only just woken up, out to the world beyond this stone home, the world from which she has somehow, for a moment, slipped.

It is the solstice, and one of us – this speckled bird, newly formed – lingers at the window, now opened, for long enough that I think, for the briefest moment, that she might settle on the nest beside her, carried in from the lane just the night before. The dog, in her confusion, has gone out the door.

One of us, heart-caught and shaken, sees the speckled wing of the other, long after the window closes, after the fledgling's trace has left the empty room. She came, and when she did, I could not keep her, that little one. Her coming in, you see, was really all it took.

Some creatures come without you even calling. They arrive, while you are sleeping, through your door. It is the solstice, and the light out there is changing. Stand and watch, now, as it bleeds out from the sky. Particular light, though, when it comes, it comes to change us. Some light, when it comes, it comes to stay.

It takes our grief and helps us sculpt it into bone. It nestles in, beside those bones, a porcelain silence. Some creatures, through their absence, bring the light.

Iúil, July

Buck Moon
Feather Moulting Moon
Thunder Moon
Halfway Summer Moon
Raspberry Moon
Ripe Corn Moon
Salmon Moon
Hay Moon
Wort Moon
Moon Where the Cherries Are Ripe

Fuinneog An Lae, Dawning light
Fuinseóg, Ash

We had known after just a handful of nights in our new home that we would need to have the ash tree taken down. We'd watched it try in vain to hold itself up, in squally, steel-grey midwinter winds, decay clinging – dry and hoary – to its towering, lifeless skeleton. Back then we watched as December had given itself over to the hungry, bitter-white fingers of winter. The isolated laneway glistened with frost in the morning, with planets and stars in the night-time. And soon a new year had arrived – nameless – a dimly lit, unknowable thing.

We knew, way back then, that we would have to wait until the storm season had passed before we could put the dead tree out of its misery, and so we huddled close to one another. The tin roof of the barn behind our house rattled like a wailing banshee, in winds that made us feel as though we were out at sea. Far, far away from that laneway, in the very heart of Ireland. We prayed to all that we both knew – and didn't – that the ash would remain upright, would not come crashing down on our hundred-year-old roof, would not make for the ground – reminding us that all will become ash, anyway, someday.

Ash can be burned from the moment you have cut it down. Druids believed it had the ability to blend masculine and feminine energy but also that it would be the first hit by lightning. If you place ash berries in a cradle, it protects the baby from being stolen by the fairies. Sailors believe that if they carry a piece of ash carved into the shape of a solar cross they will be protected from drowning. As a tree it is also closely interwoven with the idea of healing. Irish emigrants carried a piece of ash to mind them due to its power over water. It historically has been used to build boats, and as such is beloved of those married to the sea. Due to its strength and ability to grow to such great heights, it's referred to in Celtic mythology as the World Tree; a tree that spans worlds. This sense of its thinness, its role as stepping-stone between realms, might be what ties it so closely to childbirth. In many parts of the Highlands, at the birth of a child, the midwife would burn a green stick of ash, administering the sap as the first drop of liquid to the new-born child: the tree's milk delivering the very first strength to the newly born. Poorly babies would be passed naked through a cleft in an ash tree to heal them, and an intimate bond between tree and human is often spoken of. The tree in the exact heart of Ireland, at the Hill of Uisneach, one of the five great trees of Ireland, was an ash: Bile Uisnigh. The ash's ties to water, fertility and growth place it seasonally in late spring or early summer when its delicate foliage first appears.

We got the call to say that the surgeons were allowed to work again in between Irish lockdowns. We were offered only one slot. The morning before the event, starlings visited the top branches of the dead ash in vast droves. They came in their unruly, metallic numbers throughout that whole day. I remember so clearly the thick clouds of grey and lilac that held them close. The almost silence that filled that strange summer giving itself over to their murmuring, manic mayhem. I went, in the middle of these shenanigans, to meet someone I had been in touch with since before the pandemic. Another writer, one whose words feel spell-like, ancient. I sat, after the starlings, tea in hand, at the table of this person who I knew within moments of meeting would become a very important person in my life. There are some people who have been in my life for decades, in whose presence I have never mentioned the events of my early childhood, but that afternoon I spoke so freely, so trust-ingly. It felt like that type of listening was one of the greatest gifts, a stranger could ever give another. Leaving, we stood together at the front door of their home and told M about the time spent; how charged it was. How rent of energy we felt from all the emotion. How we each felt it could never have been our first meeting. I found out two days later that on that eve of the ash being taken from its place in the world, that day I'd made a close friend of a stranger, the man who'd shattered my childhood had died.

1st

Woolf's diary entry for today:
'I am in the mood to dissolve in the sky.'
Hear Hear. (Here Here.)
Rain has not stopped for weeks.
Reading Rebecca Tamas' *Strangers* and feeling so strengthened
by her words. Thinking about what it means to be in relation-
ship with every other being on earth, not just the human.
Imagining a way through (and not giving in to the sorrow and
fear that claws at my guts).

2nd

There is a kind of tiredness in me I have never before known.
If it ever goes away, I shall be immeasurably grateful. Part of
me wonders if it's our bodies, all of our blood and bone – the
parts that make us a living thing – simply trying to live through
this.

3rd

Barry Lopez's *Winter Count* has shaken me up, left me unsure
why I would ever write a word when words like those exist
in the world. "'If one is patient," he said, "if you are careful, I
think there is probably nothing that cannot be retrieved.'"
I want to learn to be patient more than any other thing.
Swam in the lough in the pouring rain, then returned home
to Anne Carson. I have never been more hungry for the cold
water. I have never been more hungry for the words of others.
Gathered, from a drenched herb garden, two types of mint,
fennel, thyme, sage and rosemary.
From the bottom of the garden – rocket, lettuce leaves and
the most exquisitely coloured edible flowers (the name escapes
me just now).

4th
Painting with pink and yellow and gold. Leaves my head calm,
for the briefest but most tender of moments.
Then – a run up a wet laneway. An attempt to shift the anger
that feels to have taken root.

5th

Full Buck Moon.

> Yellow – dipping in & out
> of thick black cloud
> – shroud-like

> dancing under
> a pinky-grey veil
> – marbled, above
> the bottom field.

> Beneath us, the
> dark, still Bog;
> full of hunger
> – full of bone,
> full of silence.

Drove to Killiney after coffee stop in Dún Laoghaire – parked
at that abandoned house to find an explosion of wild flowers
in the garden: a solitary poppy, cornflowers, fennel, etc.
The blue of the sky, the grey of the soft, singing horizon, the
pinks and silvers of the pebbles underfoot.
I needed it so much. The waves were strong and so full of the
beat of themselves, of the season, of me.
Walked tonight – lit by the glow of a single torch, the moon,
the planets – across the field to the gap between it and the
next.

Stood, in the space between, that liminal place – in near silence
– watching the full buck moon reveal herself to the world.
Looking, really looking, feels an act of deepest love.
Refusing to look away is a powerful political act.
Trying, now, to look; with everything I have.

6th

By the stove reading from a Wendell Berry book I'm about
to send to JS – about trees making 'a darkness here that heals'.
What a thought, a way to think of darkness.

7th

Trying to stay away from social media but feel so fucking lonely.
The rain hasn't stopped for so long and I miss people.
I am tired.
The garden is drowned.
It is an eternal winter.
I really, really just want to feel like myself again.

8th

At my wit's end. Cannot live with weather the like of this.

9th

A few feet from the front door, in a field I walk daily, a pine
marten – all sleek and timeless movement – passes the gate. I
cannot quite convey the way it stopped time. How it hauled
me – up and out – from a place I hadn't, till then, realised I
had fallen into.
Later, out the back – by the old railway line – to pick salad
leaves, I watched either the same or another for so long it felt
almost spell-like. All along the top of the shuck, beside the
clover, beneath the hawthorn and the house martins.
(Some days we invite it more than others.)

11th
there is only the yellow moon behind the dancing pewter
clouds /
    how it calls each moth by name /
    how it is unburying the seeds that did not grow /
    how when the winds answer back – the sea – like a
    fledgling bird, echoes.

12th
Almost otherworldly rain and surreal thunder in the heart of
Ireland as I watch image after image of blue skies and dancing
light in every other worldly place. Don't know how much
more of this blurry-lined year I can take before I take to
drumming at the bog, like a snipe.
Gathered the light for my own self.
Cosmos, sweet peas, so many poppies, cornflower, zinnia, fennel,
rosemary, mint, sage, so many more poppies.
This is light, too, I know.

14th
Again by the stove, after a day full of thick rain and glistening
starlings.
An exceptionally odd day. The starlings acted so out of sorts
– lifting up, grouping and regrouping – then breaking free, in
the most startling of manners.
The ash was due to be cut down today. Went out to seek its
permission, as is the way in old lore. Laid white rose petals and
inky blue cornflower heads into its belly, right at the place
where it is split – likely the bit it will be cut down to – but
the surgeons didn't come due to the incessant rain. After not
having frequented the tree for many months, the birds flitted
between it and the sycamore at the foot of the garden. They
were also making such clatter and chaos – bathing in vast
swathes at the guttering.

Heavy, thick rain all day. Eased only for a few stolen moments here and there. The poppies and cornflowers are so striking, and now the love-in-a-mist must be close to blooming. I am so grateful for this garden, always will be. On Instagram, so many people sharing visits to Derek Jarman's garden. I wonder when, if ever, I will make that trip. Feels surreal even to consider such things any more. Anyhow, yesterday at Baltray it felt like I imagine it might at Dungeness – greys, blues, steely hues as far as the eye reached. Scrub and wild flowers, industrial wasteland – and the beach itself – so full of tender and aching stillness. And those birds grouping together, leaving me spell-bound. As I left the sea's belly; a constellation of ringed plover.

We took them, at first, for starlings in murmuration but they glimmered – silver against the pewter sky – and we saw, the closer they dragged their dance, close enough to make out their outlines, that they weren't. Such unimaginable, echoey, haunting beauty.

Today H's mug arrived, just moments after I smashed the gorgeous brick I found on the beach and had begun to use as a candleholder. It made me think of impermanence, of objects, of my creaturely form. It made me think of my period, of blood & shedding, of making space for things weightier than anything physical could ever try to be. Then in the midst of this, totally out of the blue, my father sent me a picture of him as a wee boy, in a message so full of optimism I wept with joy. There is a certain kind of brokenness that can exist within families that leaves people without their childhood pictures, if any even existed in the first place, and it is precisely such brokenness that seems essential to try to heal from. If ever we have the gift of a child in our lives, I will take as many pictures as I can. I will print them out, find a large box, and fill it with them. I am trying, I know, to break this attachment to objects – but photographs feel different.

The silence of photographs. Their softness. The way they stroke parts of us we can't see.
Their ability to haunt. How they are ours and how they are not. How we are drawn to them. Their colours.
The ghosts we keep close.

17th
The ash came down. In the hours just before, starlings wheeled in the sky like noisy fishwives. Cannot help but feel it all means more than it does.
Planted comfrey from MM's garden in ours.

19th
MD died. Don't feel in any way how I felt, for decades, that I would.
Neither anger, nor relief.
Died early evening of 16th.
There is so much light in the garden with the ash gone.
Moths coming in such numbers as to seem almost otherworldly.

20th
6 a.m. Opened the front door to let the dog out and straight away a wren flew in. She flew around all over the place, eventually landing on the window, after having landed on M's pillow and the right-hand corner of the four-spotted moth picture. From the window, she made eye contact with me and it was unlike any moment I have ever experienced before.

Later on, around the time when MD was being placed back into the earth, the light in our garden was absolutely exquisite. It fell on the oaks & roses, on poppies blooming redder than blood. It fell on me, and on the poppies & cornflowers I have grown from seed.

What about those poppies, though? And the fresh shoots on the lavender . . . what about a world that is more miraculous than anything I have ever before imagined.

Last night we saw a comet – visible only until next month – after which it will become invisible, not to be seen again for almost 7,000 years.

(I am convinced we made our baby last night.)

21st

From 1912: 'What matters is precisely this; the unspoken at the edge of the spoken.' Woolf, who else could it be? These words, oh these words, for these days that are in it.

Galway.

The bog, the light, the heather, the lifting of the birds, the swim(s) of all the dreams, the view across to the Flaggy Shore, the greys (o! the greys) . . .

(Today I left my everything in Connemara.)

22nd

Counted, before bed, tens of moths in our small cottage.

Carried in, as the last light faded, a handful of soft red sweet peas, grown from seed, which I will never quite get over. For proper gardeners it might be no big deal, this attending to something from beginning to end. I have cared for these things from seed. Really this is too much to begin to contemplate, somehow. After a lifetime spent thinking I would break or ruin everything that I touched, now the most beautiful things I have set eyes on grow just steps from my front door. Those nigella – the white & midnight & sky of them – I nurtured into being. That sea holly right in my line of vision, the purple of it so vibrant as to be unreal – was a seed only months before today. How can any of this even be real?

Oh, the poppies, though. The peaches & oranges, the yellows & creams, the utter and unstoppable goodness of their being. Peas & kale, calendula & cauliflower, & cornflowers, so many cornflowers. I am so lucky.

This evening, in the closest one might get to silence in a house, we read to the sound of heavy rainfall.

23rd
Going so grey and I am so here for it.
Found, in the Dublin Hills when looking at a van, a set of pure-white jaw bones, which made me dive into Kathleen Jamie's *Sightlines* the second we got home, despite my sheer exhaustion.

24th
More sweet peas to try to soothe my brain.

Will this rain ever stop?
Broad beans, spring onions and fennel, gathered in waterproofs, for dinner – with lavender, roses and cornflowers just because.

25th
Kale kale kale; I am so gladdened by it today.
'Sometimes I dream a sentence and write it down. It's usually nonsense, but sometimes it seems a key to another world.'
O! the dreamed sentence, the writing of it down, keys in its teeth like rattling bones, the words of Anne Carson. (Then, as if that was not enough: Marie Howe's 'The Promise', until I could take no more.
And still this unending winter. I am spent.)
Later . . .
SOUGHT and found (a rainbow above the bog).

A crescent moon below lavender-grey clouds holds a promise that I can't fully hear.
Oh, and the first beetroot!

26th
Storm moon, last night, in a meadow with moths.
I wish I could word that hour a little better but I feel so tired. Last night, for the first time since she came, the dog cried until she got into the room with us. I was terrified there was something wrong but it seems she just wanted to lie by my bed on the floor.

Blue skies. Back to beautiful Louth, and I am so grateful to have found this coastline that already means so much to me. Coffee in flask, papers and books with the one I love. It always was, but has become even more so, about these small things. Another double dip and I am so surprised by this pull east, where before it was always north or west. We change if we allow ourselves.

20 months sober. It has included more trauma than I wish to even note down here. I thought I'd be bombarded by drinking dreams the longer the pandemic went on, but the dreams have not been that way at all. Instead I have dreamed of winged things, coming in the night – silently – and landing on my skin. I am marking this day because I need to remember that I got through this. It has been hideous at times, but I waken every day and I choose this life, and I am so unbelievably grateful.

A feather, found as the sun shone down on scalding sand, on getting out of the sea.
Shared on my stories, to the unanimous answer that it is the feather – fallen, wondrous – of a woodpecker. I am moved by

this so much, by the way it all falls so magical, otherworldly, fairytale-like. There I was dripping salt off my tired body, drinking lukewarm decaf coffee, in a place a woodpecker had – at some unknown point in the past – flown over. How can those things coexist; sit beside one another in a given moment, a given sentence?

Woodpecker-dream interpretation, as found on the internet: Like a blue-jay dream, you are being asked to pay attention to your waking life. There may be something you have overlooked, and this is bringing it back to your focus. This bird will herald the beginning of a very busy time for you but you will see it all through to completion.

27th
Love-in-a-mist, is all.
And Michael Longley.

(Last night the 1st sentence of the book came to me, dreamed as a woodpecker.)

28th
Woke up feeling deeply troubled, ridden with anxiety. It shall pass.
Happy birthday, Beatrix Potter.

29th
Read, before I even ate breakfast, Annie Ernaux's *I Remain In Darkness*.
Exquisite, ghostly creature of a thing.

30th
Galway.

Sandpiper murmuration; making me rethink the word *wildness*
– for how could my own reflect theirs in any shape at all?
  Swimming beneath the most powerful waves, reminding me
how small I am; how made of moon & bone.

31st
Eve of Lughnasadh
Four-spotted footman moth, in the bedroom, right beneath
the image of him I bought from the artist Sarah Gillespie.
The most beautiful creature to exist, visiting me, in the yellow-
grey dawn.
The voice of Virginia Woolf – like a sky-shoal of silvery plover
– from my bed.
The only flower to make me weep – love-in-a-mist – grown
from seed in ghostly days, opened up its eyes; to the thunder-
pealed, echoey sky.

After writing my first book I promised myself to put grief away and to never, ever lift it back out again.

I swore blind I'd give it no more room – in my days, my work, my world. I had sickened myself with it, as they say.
I had reached the end of its coal-black line.

Recently I read that we might know, as writers, when the work is ready, and that this moment might be as soon as we feel we cannot even look at it any more. It seems that might be how I am with my material. As soon as I have reached saturation point – as soon as I never want to hear the word again – only then should I actually be allowed to write about the thing at hand. I should never have dreamed of writing about grief before, way back then, when I was so obsessed with it as to call it a bird. When I was young and foolish and full of even more bullshit than I am now.

The blue hydrangea we carried from the Bogside in the heart of Derry, to the concrete yard of an old shirt factory inside the city's walls, to the waterside, then to this central bogland of Ireland, have died. Someone I cared for so deeply but who reciprocated with pain, loves hydrangea, and I have spent the best part of a year wondering how it is possible to still love something that holds such devastating memories for you. How to love a plant that always makes you think of a person who did not love you back? How to love a plant that makes you think of all the things that have been thrown at you? How still to love a thing that holds your trauma in its very roots? That knows your grief as intimately as it knows the soil?

A poet I so deeply admire tweets an Emily Dickinson quote about mud and I am rapt – taken by the words in ways I struggle to make sense of. I google 'gardening Emily Dickinson' and the first return is a National Endowment for the Humanities site, an iconic image of her – black and white, the flower in her hands ginkgo-yellow, although I instantly recognise it as hydrangea. To the left, the following words: 'In her own time she was better known for her hydrangeas.' The article goes on to tell me that fewer than a dozen of her poems were published before her death. The people living close to the poet would, in fact, have known her as a gardener.

A solitary woman, by lantern light, tending to her garden, dressed in white,
   'I was reared in the garden, you know,' she wrote to her cousin just before she turned 30. Yes, I think, this is the way the world should work. I want to rear my child in a garden. I want to rear myself in one, too. I want to let the muck and dirt get in under all the skin and fix things, to fix everything. I want to start loosening myself from the hold of a past that does not serve me, that never did.

My lover comes into our bedroom – I am tucked in beneath the sheet already, bone-tired from the garden, mud still beneath my nails – and tells me, as though it were the thing of most importance in all the world: 'Emily Dickinson was a gardener.'
   He tells me that her poem 'There is another sky' – written for her brother – holds the garden up as a bringer of hope in hard times. He has heard this on the radio, just before bed, and it has struck him as something he knows will touch me, so he carries the words into me in one hand, a mug made by a friend not quite full of the Pukka night-time tea he makes me each evening, without fail, in the other.

I fall asleep listening to Josephine Foster sing the words of that poet-gardener with the window wide open to my own garden.
   My first garden.

The place I shall think of, always and evermore, when I hear the word *garden*.

To tend to a garden is to remove, to take away so much more than we could ever imagine, to make room for all that still will come.

Growing is about order, it strikes me.

About the intentional clearing of space by cutting things back.

To tend a garden is to free ourselves from the things we long have known should have no place in our lives & in our days (& in our gardens).

I wish I'd known, long before now,
that sowing is a way to grieve.

As hands scatter seeds
into earth beneath feet,
they are really sculpting loss.

With careful, repeated movements,
the hands are moulding it,
into a thing like light on stone.

Derek Jarman.
Virginia Woolf.
Alice Oswald.
William Morris.
Jamaica Kincaid.
Barbara Hepworth.

Everyone I am drawn to is a gardener,
although I think I only realised it this year.

My closest friend sends me words that feel like the only words
that I might ever need again for the rest of my days – written
on the envelope that holds her own words inside – lovingly
jotted down in between the giving of love, the wiping of tears,
the boiling of blood oranges, the movement of tired limbs that
make up her day: 'Love needs no planting, it is sown by seed.'
These envelope words are by Louise Erdrich, from a book
called *The Blue Jay's Dance*. I google it, having heard of it before
but not having ever encountered it – to find it is a book about
mothering (of course it is). I promise myself that I will read
it, no matter the outcome of the weeks and months ahead.
That I will let go of the idea that there is, constantly, some
gathering to which I have not been invited. I know, so deep
inside me that I can't quite separate it from my guts, that this
is not the way motherhood works. I know I belong there, too,
and to some extent we all do.

Every single one of us belongs in that wild garden.

'To protect what is wild is to protect what is gentle.
Perhaps the wilderness we fear is the pause between our
own heartbeats, the silent space that says we live only by
grace. Wilderness lives by this same grace.'
                                        Terry Tempest Williams

I wake with a fierce desire on me, hauled from sleep by imme-
diacy, by yearning, the want upon me, like the wolf. In the
Irish language no one is said to *be* the emotion they are feeling
in any given moment. I spend an inordinate amount of time
trying to word this line better but fail, decide instead to show

in place of telling – as it were. In Irish, no one is ever sad, angry; heartbroken, joyful, terrified, hopeful. All of this, this inexhaustible list of ways of being in the world, simply become cloaks that one might hang upon a wooden peg fastened to the back of a bedroom door. Right there, on top of your silk floral kimono – the one bought for a fiver in a Stoke Newington charity shop the last summer you spent single, one you learned to visibly mend on a group Zoom call organised by Toast, a handful of months into a global pandemic – hangs sorrow. You take it down from its resting place, draw it in near to you so you smell its fibres, then put it on. There it is, on top of a silk pale-peach blouse – sorrow.

Sorrow is upon you and will remain so only for as long as need be. You are not sorrowful, you understand, as you continue about your day. As you try to do all the things you need to do in order to convince those around you that all is well, that you are well. Rather, as you try to convince those around you that instead of sorrow being upon you that day, there is one of the other cloaks instead. You try to allow the emotions to simply be, to ride over you like a wave; to linger on your skin like woodsmoke, to come & go as they please like a season or an old wandering creature that was never even once yours.

Promise this to yourself: I am not the way I feel.

I'm interested to find, upon further unravelling, that when someone says they are sorry in Irish, what they actually say is that there is sorrow somewhere on their being. That the very act of apologising is an acknowledgment of the impact a given action, word, or other transgression has had on the one who carried it out.

Tá brón orm, Sorrow is upon me.

Anyway, enough about language and its slippery, self-flagellating ways.

Back to desire.

Back to that desire I seem to have awoken with; its thick-pelted body on top of my own creamy, salty one.

The desire to write – only and obsessively – about colour.

I tell myself this is something of which I have no real under-standing, so must steer clear of – only to realise I have gone down this very route before. I have written (I have tried to) about colour countless times before. Like light, its glistening, haunting bedfellow, it is a thing from whose hold I cannot quite manage to loosen myself.

I wonder what it means, this urge, this ache in me, but my brain feels too frazzled to go through the steps.

Instead, I beg myself to step back, to move to the side, to close my ears as the following colours call to me, insistent as lovers: apricot, fallow, light periwinkle, amber, ghost-white, battleship-grey, mantis, bud-green, robin-egg blue, orange peel, celadon, earth-yellow, corn silk, mulberry, dogwood rose, old lace, saffron, pistachio, umber, sage, thistle, winter sky.

To give in to this call will leave me hungry for other people, other places, other times. I have had my fill, this year, of longing. I need to live as fully as I can in the colours that fill my days here and now, come what may.

I tell myself that this colour yearning will only be upon me for a short while. Soon, before the day is out I hope, I will lift it over my tired head, fold it as neatly as I can and find a place to put it. A basket on a shelf high enough that I cannot hear their calls – these colours – as I try, with all my might, to sleep. A place far enough away that I can try to forget the way it feels to arrive somewhere you have never before been. As night begins to fall, the daytime colours of the place begin to loosen around the edges, and the colours of the night begin to stretch out their long limbs. As the earth and the sky of this strange, shifting place begin — quietly, then with a force not unlike thunder — to name their unfamiliar hues.

I give in to sleep, and find myself in a bright, walled garden, full of colour and what at first might be mistaken for silence.

It is late summer.

Birds, with quiet regularity,
are moving about the space,
here to there, and back again.

Everywhere, nests.
Everywhere, creatures.
Everywhere, light.

Trees sway softly in a breeze only just there.
I realise, even as I try to navigate the dream's
boundaries, that this garden is – to put it
simply – my everything.
This garden is those nests that came and
stayed, that light that came and stayed.

This garden – no matter how different it
looks in a dream – is the garden right outside
my door.

This garden is the making of me,
and don't I know it.

Lúnasa, August

Sturgeon Moon
Harvest Moon
Grain Moon
Red Moon
Fruit Moon
Ricing Moon
Lightning Moon
Flying Up Moon
Moon When the Cherries Turn Black
Mountain Shadows Moon

What was your first dream?

The one that taught you what it meant to be asleep. What it meant to leave your daytime shell behind. The one that taught you that the night was yours and yours alone?

When one of my parents met their first partner after my other parent, I began, for the first time, to experience something that a number of women in my bloodline had before me. I began to have 'seeing dreams'. This new adult in my life, one who looked to almost all the other adults in my life to be a very likeable person indeed, began to come to me in dreams as the person they would end up showing themselves as, as soon as they moved in with my parent. They chased me through wild, dark mazes, they took their plethora of masks on and off in alleyways and covered my mouth to keep me quiet. They laughed at me when I cried and told me they were taking my parent away. I woke from these dreams unsure what to do with these things that my mind was doing to me as I slept.

In my teenage years I dreamed of – on two occasions – people dying, a handful of days before they did. Neither of them had been unwell at the time. I dreamed of separations, of falls that happened, and of a single crash that came – for everyone else involved – out of nowhere. I dreamed of a house move and a house loss, of illness and coupling, I dreamed of floods and of birds that nested in the least likely of locations – all before the things happened in the 'real' world.

Recently I was asked for a piece to speak a little to what dreams meant to me. What images – if any – were recurrent. How close the relationship was between my dream life and my writing. Answering it almost broke my heart, and I do not mean that to be taken lightly. I thought back, over and over (and for far too long afterwards), on how rich – how magical, in fact – my dream life had been in the past. Not in relation to the dreams of which I have just spoken, those ones that, if I am honest, left me scared and unsure who was safe to share such things with. Rather, in relation to the regular, run-of-the-mill dreams, those that would turn up on random nights when I was least expecting them, full of phantastic, cavorting magic.

A small, inexhaustible list:

The River Foyle
(frozen, shallow, bottomless, purple, full of bodies, littered with
poetry on scraps of paper
etc., etc., etc.)
Whales, bells, a xylophone, too many winged creatures to even
begin to mention.
Skulls, dancing planets, the tall, thin cans of Fanta from the
late eighties.
Themoonthemoonthemoonthemoonthemoon.
Trees & drugs. Snow & chlorophyll. Storms & islands.
Humans & more than.
Babies & lost species. Crows holding the world between their
beaks. Salmon-pink skies on other planets. Gardens upon
gardens upon gardens.
The sea. Always, and endlessly, the sea.

Are we dreaming more in this surreal, seemingly unending year?
Are we dreaming differently?
Has this time changed our creative landscape, the one we set sail for as our eyes close, and we bid the day goodbye?

My lover has a somewhat peculiar relationship with his dreams. Even writing this sentence feels silly, the words misshapen. How do I know what is peculiar? How can any of us try to wrangle with the working of the mind in the velvety dark? Anyhow – peculiar or not – each morning, since the very first one on which we woke up together, I have asked him if – and of what – he dreamed. No matter the season, no matter the setting, no matter the circumstance, his response takes one of three shapes.

He did not dream.

He dreamed but he cannot find them in the harsh light of morning.

He dreamed and he unravels it for me as he would a tangled piece of rope.

The first was much more common in the early days of our love, and for many moons I worried myself sick that what this really meant was that he had dreamed (and could easily find them despite the light) but that he had no desire to share them with the like of me. Soon I began to understand this was a part of him I had to simply let be.

I cannot remember if I have ever told him the dream that I am recalling, for it occurred in a time before him.

The Dream That I Am Recalling / Hummingbird

Early summer is the season, an unrevealed Scottish island is the setting for this, the dream that I am recalling. This dream that I am recalling is all bright white light and dappled glimmerings. It is all hazy as a morning lost to love, or illness, or grief. It is full of much that is unknown, this dream that I am recalling. I stand at the top of the garden path, a tall sycamore in front of me, a yellow door behind me, watching as the dream unearths itself right before my tired eyes. I am root-bound. I am hungry. I am anxious and unsure how the memory will land in me, what trace it might leave behind. I watch the younger, dream-me enter a copse – a sparse clearing within a crowded evergreen forest – and I wonder immediately if the location might be the Isle of Mull. She walks around, this girl, in a circle. She has never been here before, but she acts as though she has, somehow. She is eager. She is thin. She is alone. The dream is on a loop. The same motion, the same circle, the same quietude. Until it breaks. The quiet breaks, and the dream gallops towards an even greater unknown. She is no longer alone. She knows it in her core but she is far from shaken. A bird has entered the circle and it is flying backwards. It is parakeet green and flamingo pink. It is kingfisher blue and it is flashes of bird colour she is oblivious to. It hovers. It is never still. It feels like a dream within a dream: ekphrasis. She is even less alone than before. All at once, an old man enters the loop. He is blond. He is gentle. He is alone.

'*You have a choice to make. You can return, go back to where you started out from, and record this bird you have discovered, put its name down in ink. Or you can stay with it a little longer, draw in close, look – really see – the bird. But you cannot do both. You can never do both, you see.*'

I waken from this dream that I am recalling – to find the rooftops outside my window hidden from view, the tenements all stolen away by snow that wasn't forecast – that came without warning, that left just as it arrived.

A thief in the night; a fox amongst the chickens.

1st

Lughnasadh, the beginning of the harvest season.

The circle turning. What might these next months hold for us all? I don't really want to try to imagine, I don't want any more hopes being scuppered, happier living in the day-to-day of it all, as best I can.

Everywhere is pink and full of wren-song.

Sat on front doorstep, sun peeking (trying to) through thick grey storm clouds. Birds fluttering about and singing. M taking apart the concrete steps. Grass, yet again, being cut. Strong winds rustling the trees and the roses. Cannot quite bring myself to believe it's August. What a surreal aul' year. I've shifted the direction the milking-stool is facing, now I'm beneath a small patch of blue sky that's been hung above the field. To the right of my foot lavender in my favourite terracotta pot. To my left, ahead of me, the patch of wild flowers I was convinced stood no chance of flowering. Californian poppies – the orange & peach of them so perfect, so delicate but strong – love-in-a-mist, my absolute favourites now; cornflowers – so many, in so many different shades of blue – and I'm affected by them. By their presence, their very existence, in ways I'm not sure if I can word. Communicating things such as resilience, seeds, hope, giving myself over to all that may never come – or that (against all odds) might indeed come: these are early steps I'm taking. These words. Getting back, step by step, to trying to find a routine for myself.

It is starting, a little, to rain. Small specks of it, like sparks from a fire, are landing on my skin.

I have finished the review for *Suppose a Sentence*, Brian Dillon's excellent book 'reminding us why we should care'. Now to the acknowledgments for TP. I am anxious even thinking of starting. Where to begin? What a huge task, to thank all those who allowed your first book to be moulded into being. So deeply grateful.

2nd
Lankum, as loud as it'll go, early in the morning.
Joyjoyjoyjoy (first car-boot sale in over seven months!) and the light is finally back.
Found: a white & blue enamel candleholder, a wee wooden thing that tells you when it is Friday, Saturday, Sunday or none of these (blank), an exquisite, rusted, cream enamel bucket (first Irish enamelware I ever have found), a wooden-handled trowel, a pale blue enamel mug.
Then – back to bed in larklight – more tired than ever I have known. Within moments, the heaviest of rain, falling on all the roofs, of all the buildings, all around.
Before bed – a pale pistachio-green candle in the new holder. Last light, on last night before the moon is full.

3rd
John Hume.
We will never, ever forget.
Lost for words.

4th
Asked to write some words for the *Irish Times*.
How could any of us even begin to speak of John Hume?
I recall that story of the funeral at which a woman who had lost a family member told him she prayed he would bring about peace so no other family had to suffer in that way. He listened and he wept. Less than a year later, the first steps towards lasting peace were taken. Every single time anyone ever asks: 'What kind of a man cries?' I think: 'The kind of man that brings peace to a land in need of healing.'

Agnes Martin for the whole long afternoon. 'The mystery of beauty, the truth and reality are all the same.'

5th
A white feather found on the shoreline, for JH.
Not quite sure how this has happened, but I think I have fallen in love with the east coast.
After a day full of torrential rain, a blue sky at Blackrock that would make you weep.

6th
Brilliant conversation between Esther Kinsky and Caroline Schmidt on gardens – for Women in Translation month. The short-lived, delicate nature of poppies and how perhaps that makes them the more beautiful.
Publication day for *Antlers of Water* which I adored.
U loaned me *In Praise of Shadows*, which I devoured after supper. Utterly perfect in every way.

7th
Torrential rain, icy breeze and Rilke. 'The uncertainty out there, this flickering world' . . . oh my.
The first tomatoes! And kale & chard, viola & nasturtium.

Tonight, before bed, the blue & yellow of the day parted ways so peacefully it felt like the ending of more than just a single day, like the beginning of a new world, somehow. Moths hung in the small gap in between, of course, to remind me that it was – in fact – real. Not a dream, merely the ending of an ordinary, quiet day.

8th
Article in the *Guardian* on being a black mother by Sisonke Msimang really fucking moved me. 'I pay attention to my

children. I pay attention to children . . . To be a black mother is to manage the rage of others while growing joyous black children. This is no easy task.' What can be done to fix this broken world?

Stood beneath a sky hung with more light than I've ever known – sent from times & places & others – that echo down – like the call of that night bird, aligning itself with the whirring of wings, dusty, ghostly, and the moon with its delicate bones, softly cracked.

[everything is going to be OK]

Listening to folk talk on the radio about JH and unable to stop the tears from coming. Unsure if any of us could ever fully say how important what he gave us was.
Triple-dip day. Body in the blue three times, after so long without. And so many swifts. Joy.
Gloaming harvest: one of each colour of the sweet peas, and two soft grey feathers.

9th
'Now thats an odd reflection – how one's relation with a person seems to be continued after death in dreams, and with some odd reality too.' Woolf, of course.

Dreamed of watching moths & night birds, butterflies & doves in a planet-lit, pale-yellow field, from a slowly moving, lantern-soft train carriage, in a summer both later, & earlier, than this one.
Caitlín Maude, translated by Doireann Ní Ghríofa, in bed, and more Woolf (*A Room of One's Own*). Then *A Musical Offering* – which I am utterly obsessed with. 'Even a foetus dreams. And it can only dream in sounds: the beating heart of its mother

... Silence is the mother's heart beating. Sound, whether dreaming or awake, is the mother's heart beating.'

10th
First proper day away in many months.
Listened, on the journey, to Edwyn Collins.
11 collared doves, on the grey, at the old manse.
Connemara, in the full sun of summers long passed by, o, o.
First swim with ringed plover, then read Woolf.
Second with a cormorant and arctic tern.
Gathered pebbles for the garden.
Last swim of the day was beneath a murmuration (?) of sand-pipers that painted the clouds silver.
Bought test at Salthill.

11th
Poipín

Stood just now in my first garden, surrounded by the poppies I grew from seed, with a creature inside me the size of a poppy seed.

Back to bed, shattered beyond compare, head full of oh so much, then I hear the beat of something both bigger and smaller than me, in the other room. Not one house martin but two, for the first time, encircling the space of our wee home. I don't know what these beauties are telling me, but oh my, am I listening.
The newest white rose is in bloom, the older one has turned red?!
Sat beside them both, beneath a full sun, reading *The Republic of Motherhood*; as if for the very first time. 'Inside me you pulsed, / single celled, / extraordinary.' Oh heart of mine.

Glorious package arrived from B in Barton Books. Oh
Penzance!
Garlic-bread pizza and pasta for dinner with the doors flung
open wide, as the sun set in a pink but reddening sky.

12th
Dreamed of the white cliffs of Dover but instead of horror
there was hope, like a winged creature, waiting to greet those
arriving from the hardest journey of their lives. (Reading *This
Tilting World*, again.)

My grandfather is gone seven years: a full cycle of cells &
blood. I have wanted, almost daily for this whole unreal year,
to be able to talk with him – even if it had to be in the middle
of a muddy field on WhatsApp, as I've had to with everyone
else. How I would love to call him up and tell him: 'Look,
Pappa, look at how I got through. How I managed so much
more than mere survival. Look how I have learned to be *living*.'
Every single day I want to call him and tell him I planted a
garden, that the poppies are for him. And to thank him for
telling me to wait for the right one, and that he came. How
I wish he could have met M. How they would find so much
to admire in one another. Today, of all days, the fledglings are
learning to fly.

Struggling to sleep, head full of thoughts about trigger-
warnings for TP. Am I worrying too much because of all the
emotion these last days, or is it valid?

13th
When we talk of you, we try not to get too hopeful. We try
to dance the most delicate dance I've ever known – between
hope and strength. I'm not sure why but I am convinced you
will come to us. I wonder if it is this conviction that has me

writing to you – as though we've already met – as though,
already, and for quite some time – I have held you as close to
me as a person can hold another. Today we (this word means
you and I, now) walked along on the east coast, beneath cormor-
ants and gannets with your dadda. A petrol-blue sky, golden
grasses, soft sands. The sun high above us, shining down. Then
I swam beneath a steel-grey sky full of birds at Baltray. My first
swim after discovering I am pregnant, full of the knowledge
that it will never be just me again. I worry, already, about the
loss of my independence . . . what this all might mean for my
identity, then instantly feel guilty. Message with L, who tells me
all motherhood is a form of grief, promises I will manage. Then
the sky turned pinky-grey, and we stopped for ice cream at
Castlepollard on our way home. These days everything feels so
achingly precious I could weep (and often I do).

'This tilting world, how can we talk about it, how to make
sense of it?' Colette Fellous, translated by Sophie Lewis; what
a book.

14th
Grey again today but I'm basking, still, in the leftover light of
yesterday.

Woke up remembering that deeply moving experience yesterday
in storm-warmed waves, with a half-moon rising. Just us (three)
and the dog on that vast, beautiful stretch of eastern coast,
where the land gives itself over to the sea. How I gathered
two white shells and held them up to the ebbing silence. How
I went, when we got home, straight to bed, bone-tired and
full of borrowed light, to a dream of my lover carrying a delicate, exquisite bird skull, from a snowy laneway, into our wee

grey house – and placing it silently into my hands, as I lay in our warm wooden bed.

Baby the size of an orange seed. Not sure why this feels so massive.

Thought, immediately I learned this, of Louis MacNeice's tangerine and roses, his utterly perfect 'Snow': 'There is more than glass between the snow and the huge roses' . . .

Roses in bloom again. It feels like the garden knows (how utterly ridiculous).

15th

Severe insomnia.

Today we were told it would rain all day.

Instead: blue skies and blistering sun.

The colour in the garden is riotous, unstoppable.

I read for the whole day, as well as thinking of you.

Your da' thinks you will be a girl. Oh my.

The robin was in the house this morning, and I think perhaps there are eggs in the house martin's nest beside the yellow door.

Sweet peas & lavender, calendula & phacelia, cosmos & cornflowers – and poppies, of course – gathered at sunset and brought into our wee house. The reminder that the joy of existence can never be too far from our hands, no matter what form it may take. (I forgot to say love-in-a-mist. How could I? It is divine, with heads looking like they will remain over winter, sculptural bringers of joy on dark, cold days.)

Julia Kerninon on the art and act of writing: 'To possess a wooden table that I could work at in the peaceful morning light, to have enough money to feed my children, enough time to love whomever I would love' – oh sweet heart of mine, yes! For lunch – dhal, with lashings of edible flowers; what pure joy.

16th

Helen Hooker O'Malley, and soft roses – peach, pink, cream, red and white – as I feed the starter for today's bread.
Fierce, storm-grey sea & sky, in Wicklow.
Choppy, gorgeous swim at the Forty Foot.
An egret, in the silt, as we walked with A.
Sleep still refuses to come. Spent two hours looking back at old pictures of the dog when we first met her and crying.
Hormones makes love act differently, these days.

17th

Severe migraines without pain relief are quite something.
Tipping down again. Working from bed.
A perfect meadow brown, on my hand, for so long it felt almost unreal.
Such a wet, wild night. Felt so glad the house martins are all snug in the nests they've built outside our home.

18th

Broke the replacement candleholder J got me when I broke the one L gave me.
Clumsy beyond words, just now, and so tired.

19th

Received, in the quiet afternoon, the first proof of TP.
I can't even nearly find the words.

20th

Took to bed very early last night with the most horrific migraine that has yet to pass.

21st

Struggling to find a doctor. Hope to sort one soon.

The dog, as soon as M leaves to get the things we need, is straight in to mind me. She knows, of that I am certain. Still not keeping food down but managed to leave bed to sit by stove with Olga Tokarczuk's *Flights* and ginger tea.

22nd
Woke up missing L & IM more than I thought possible to miss anyone.
Baby now the size of a sweet pea. Our sweet peas in no hurry to stop. Can't keep up with cutting them.
Sent some home with P for his mam with a copy of *Winter Papers*. He was beaming.

23rd
Woke up somewhere else for the first time in seven months. Surreal.
There's a mountain behind the fog.

Happy birthday Mister Edwyn Collins. Some man for one man.
Home to our beautiful garden in whispering evening light.

24th
It's always going to be a good day when a fledgling house martin lands on the bed with you, as calm as can be.
Back in bed, contemplating this wild unknown, with all its haunting beauty.
Too tired to say any more.

25th
no echo ~ no echo ~ no echo ~ no echo
(Woolf, and her 'furnace behind the sky', of course . . .)

And an unidentifiable pearlescent moth in the sunless afternoon.
Then – horseshoes & apples & eclipses.

26th
UP WITH THE LARKS (again).
Spent the early morning with the new *Willowherb Review* and
a punnet of raspberries, then off to Mayo to look at a van.
Swam in the most powerful Atlantic waves of my life then
listened to Edwyn Collins. Both these seemingly ordinary things
now leave me bawling my eyes out, which they never did
before this year. Not sorrow, not joy: I think it's being alive,
just.

(We bought the van.)

27th
Freezing, wet and wild all day. So glad to be by the hearth.
Feel like only now am I growing to understand what is going
on, the changes that are at work inside my body & my days
& our lives. We are going to have a baby. I am in the wildest
place I might ever know. Only giving birth, if I am that lucky
to get there, feels like it could be wilder than pregnancy. Never
in a million years did I think I would be here, that this would
happen for us. And so quickly. So long spent grieving for
something that would never be, only to have it come along in
the most odd, unthinkable period of my entire life . . .
M asked, as we drank our coffee, how I felt about it all, if I
was OK, and I struggled to name the feelings. The truth is
there are some I think I never have felt before but there are
some I know so well in beside the strangers. Gratitude, worry,
disbelief and pure joy are dancing inside my belly all at once,
which is a cocktail I have not really tasted before. The life that
is ahead – of me, of M, of us both – is in an entirely changed
form from what I always imagined it would be, which is both
brilliant and terrifying all in one. Who am I now? I need to
allow myself to go back to longing. Who am I now? I need

to let myself imagine softness, once more, to leave room for vulnerability in perhaps its purest form.

28th
Baltray. Swimming under steel grey, and clouds of oystercatchers, in storm-warmed white waves.

Chips, beans and onion rings in Drogheda. Date-night of dreams in the new world.

Then home to the most glorious of all sunsets this evening. Unsure why but at the exact moment it began, I remembered the fact we were told we'd be able to travel by Easter. Heading, now, into the darker part of the year, and can't see things changing any time soon. Feeling grateful to be able to feel safe, something we all deserve but sadly don't all experience.

29th
Pancakes and *Essayism*.

The eggs have hatched, and the wee house martins are gorgeous. M chainsawed, hand-sawed, axed and sorted the ash, placing it in a dry frame he built himself. Will be ready by next year. It is on the spot from which the tree was taken down, which feels so right.

Winter is coming.

30th
Klee's *Persian Nightingales*, after another sleepless night.
Then autumnal light and birdsong.
And white circles dancing on the bedroom wall.

Seamus Heaney. 7 years today.
I miss him, and his healing words, in this world.

31st
Fierce busy morning on the feeders.
Galway with the most handsome man I know.
We sat outside Neachtains and drank coffee!
We ate at Kai! How is that real?
Big waves. Freezing cold swim.
(Everything is going to be OK.)

I'm not quite sure how it happened but – having only before ever read her words under force, for an undergrad English literature degree, half my life ago – I have found myself, in the thick of a global pandemic, utterly obsessed with Virginia Woolf. More specifically: with her journals. I find myself searching for ways by which to mark the passing of time. Neither *this* time – nor *my* time, at all, it should be noted; rather, the hours & days, the season-seeped months & the circling years – of others. Even more specifically, still: I am hungry for accounts of time experienced by *women*. Women who feel – for the very first time, as though they are calling my name – accompanied by the ringing of a small, almost silent bell. I want to unearth time's entrails, as though it were an insect I had stood on in the artless, unintentional act of simply passing through. I want to know that there have been times – countless droves of them – a chaotic, cacophonous constellation – exactly like this one, before. I want proof that this moment through which we are living is just a trick of mirrors & smoke, of circus acts & kaleidoscopes. I want to find the words that tell me when it all might end.

Time has become a thing all of its own curious, untameable making. For the first time in my life, perhaps, an event is coming towards me which will act as a stone placed in the damp, ancient earth. A marker in the landscape. A dot on the chart, after which point nothing might ever feel (or be) the same as before. It does not feel real, any of it. The surreal outline that the world outside has taken since spring 2020 arrived in the northern hemisphere adds to the silky, shadowy sense of it all. Nothing is real, not a single jot of it. We are wee paper birds, hung above the firmament, as a wild, untameable wind makes a choreography of our porcelain bones. It may have all begun in spring, but every single day of this ghostly, dream-like year has felt like winter, like those days on which the fog arrives, refusing – over and over – to leave.

In the past, when I was a drinker, the exquisite, melancholic dreams I had once experienced (before fiercely lunged addiction set in) stopped completely. I never really grasped, until I stopped drinking, that alcohol had stolen away my dreams. That maybe it had drowned them. That maybe they had trickled out through the broken window of my old flat on Glengyle Terrace – overlooking the frosty Meadows of Edinburgh and the ancient, pinky-red mornings of Arthur's Seat. I pictured them shapeshifting, being sculpted, like the sleepy volcano, into a part of the landscape, just outside my light-filled, hangover-tinged room. I left my dreams in Scotland, on a morning thick with haar – blown in from the sea, and vast, unnameable grief – blown in from too many days to even try to map. There is no lyrical metaphor at play here . . . After a lifetime of dazzling, dancing dreams – of hummingbirds & whales, moons & witches, colours & melody, light & words & blood & teeth & bones & loss & fishermen & islands & on & on & on – it ALL. JUST. STOPPED.

I awoke one Scottish winter's morning, seasick, with wine-red teeth, to find my nights had become a series of bobbing, emptied vessels, in a dark and desolate void.

When the pandemic first hit, I scrolled through tweet after tweet, WhatsApp after WhatsApp, article after article and so on and so on, each documenting the ways in which people's dreams had now become so vivid. Folk who had not dreamed for years, for decades, alas! – now were awakening in the dawn of any given day – to a cinematic, folkloric, heart-achingly beautiful play of the light. Scenes like those from an old magic lantern series filled their sleep, like fading photographs found in a bustling flea-market, like every childhood memory of splendour and grace they had ever thought they'd long lost. I, on the other hand, experienced nothing of the sort.

I continued to lose myself in Woolf.

In words thrown out on the stormiest of seas a century before. On the ritualistic recording of each passing day. Despite the cycle carrying on, as though nothing, whatsoever, had changed at all, in fact.

Some say they knew when they began to awaken, much earlier, or much later than they should – than they had before that first morning – and insist that *every* morning thereafter their mouths & tongues & teeth felt as though they'd spent the moonlit hours grinding on metal.

Others say they lost their sense of balance. Became, in the early light of soft dawn, disorientated; like the night had tipped them upside down, inside out, twisted all askew.

Many could not, in fact, even get up at all. Sickness like the ending of days, a headache like the moment before entering the eye of the storm; unrecognisable to their own shaken, altered selves.

I had begun, again, in those Woolf days, to record my *own* days . . . Not merely with an eye to moulding them into something for publication – a set of words that would become an object I would have to give away – but in the ways that I had always done before. In the before that existed long before last spring. In a *before* that is at least a decade before *this* time. I had begun journaling again, in the same ways I had before the world had metamorphosed into a thing I could not recognise. It is important for me to put across to you that there are other *befores* that exist long before the moments just before the pandemic. When these daily words came back again, I wept. I howled & bawled like a fur-covered creature. The rhythm and the ritual of it all – the carving of space for my inner thoughts, in the thick of such stormy chaos – felt such an act of devotion that I whined & moaned at the moon

Then, in the middle of it all, in the thick of a world so emptied of daily change, so steeped in a constant, invariable monotony, I suddenly knew that something had dragged me outside the colourless, wearisome rhythm of the everyday. Somehow, despite everything that was piled up against it, I knew that something had slipped from that world of fog & myth & longing, into this one, of blood & cells & growing.

I knew when I awoke, in a hazy pink room,
sunlight creeping in through cracks in unseen places;
silence echoing all around.

When I heard tapping on misty glass, hooded crows begging to be let inside – as fog filled every nook and cranny.
I knew when I pulled back the curtains immediately to find: no birds.
No beak marks.
No sign of fog at all in the world outside my light-dappled, moth-soft home.

I awoke one summer's day, a decade and a half after being told my body was too broken to carry such a thing – and I knew that something was growing inside me.

Something that had (somehow, against all the odds) carried my dreams back to me.

Where do I go from here, with these dreams & this change & this deep unsettling?

Where do I go from here?
Where do I even *begin?*

Meán Fomhair, September

Yellow Leaf Moon
Autumn Moon
Fruit Moon
Nut Moon
Barley Moon
Calf Moon
Rutting Moon
Corn Moon
Mating Moon
Moon When the Rice Is Laid Up to Dry
Moon When the Plums Are Scarlet
Falling Leaves Moon
Child Moon

We have lived, M and I, in this single-roomed cottage together for nine months. We could, in this time, have grown a baby. There is only a little less than this time-period left ahead of me in which I will do exactly that – if all works out. If everything is OK. If the wee seed inside me stays, grows, *becomes*. Nine months is not really a measurable, definable thing, I now understand. Nine months of what, of where, of who? Can I recall any other nine-month period in my life that acted as such a stand-alone unit? No, it seems I cannot. I try – read back through reams of handwritten journal entries – in search of a time, any time – that felt at all like this one, but I fail. Academic years fall, more or less neatly, into such a segment of a year but somehow none – not a single year of school, of university, of Waldorf Teacher Training – jumps out as feeling, in any way, shape or form – like how these nine months have felt.

I wonder (of course I do) how the nine months ahead will feel in comparison. If nothing goes wrong, I will be in the fourth trimester of motherhood. I have, only just, set foot inside the first. I glance from my queasy sickbed to the beautiful shelf M built me to keep my current books on. It is so fine an object, the wood cut, sanded, shaped and painted for me, by the person I love the most of all. A steel-grey stripe across its top matches the following things in our small room: a candle, this week's pillowcases, my linen kimono, one of the pebbles gathered from Connemara the day we found out we were going to have a baby, M's long-sleeved, washed-out cotton top, two of the stones found in St Ives last summer, the year before the world changed colour for ever. On this grey-striped wooden shelf, with its copper wire hanger, facing out to the rest of the room, are these: a brand new, unread copy of Liz Berry's *The Republic of Motherhood* (sent before we even began to try for the baby, before we had even found the words with which to

begin) from L with the following words: 'For the Mother you
already are'. A well-loved copy of Alice Oswald's *Dart* – even
the blue of it, caught from the corner of my eye, soothes me
in ways I have no real understanding of. I will not even attempt
to communicate how a book by someone I have never met
has helped me through the trickiest of times, how it has taken
the place – at various stages of my life – of mother, lover,
teacher, friend. You see, I feel like you understand this, somehow.
Perhaps of this exact book, or another by her, or perhaps
without ever having read or even heard of her – still you
understand what it is that I am trying to share. You have your
own writer(s), your own book(s). I certainly have others, too,
but right now it is all about that beautiful grey shelf. At this
moment in time when I hold, inside my tired, growing body
– a stranger I already love more than words. More than books
– the reading of, the owning of, the coveting of, the writing
of – etc. Right now, it is purely about the books that keep
me company, lying on my left side (the one I'd never once
slept on out of choice before pregnancy) as I try to ease the
queasiness with peppermint, the migraine with lavender, the
anxiety with books. Always words. Always the words of others.
This pregnancy will always be the moment (the last one?)
when I finally gave myself over to reading as long into the
night as my exhaustion would allow. When I allowed myself
to read, over and over, the books that deliver – again and again
– sustenance. Yes I am still reading for work, still reading new
words that have never crossed my eyes before, but I crave the
old words as though they were medicine – herbs that my body
needs. And so there is also a copy of *Braiding Sweetgrass*, a
dog-eared copy of *Modern Nature* and a handful of things I
own (pamphlets, poetry, writing about art and a book I will
not try to define) by women who mother and write in such
ways it feels like these two things could be carefully and happily

woven together. Books that make me feel like there might be a way to exist after this wee one comes that is not a million miles away from how I try to exist now.

Yes, these books are the objects I need to keep close to me as I sleep these days. These and that moth, the most exquisite piece of art I ever have set eyes on, made by an artist who gave birth around the same time I was born. I feel less alone in it all with these things close by. I feel less alone in the world, in my work, in my body, in myself. These small things have become so much more crucial in my day-to-day existence this year, and I am certain I am not alone.

We are changed.
We are changing, still.

I ask myself more and more these days what it might be that we need to keep us grounded in these uncertain times. When what I should really be asking is what do *I* need? It starts there, of course. We can only support those around us when we ourselves are in a safe, stable place. Past journals tell me that I have been wondering for quite some time if we are learning now to find beauty and comfort in small, everyday things. Am I, though, no matter what everyone else is up to? Because I know that is the crux of it, you see. *I* need to learn stillness. To view life as much simpler than I did before. But who among us is in a position to give in to such simplicity? Which of us gets to take that path? The language of it all, like the language of what we are living through, fails me.

I stutter and go silent again (oh how sick I am of silence. How sick I am of staying quiet.)

1st

Again & again & again – Sinéad Gleeson's *Constellations*.
'Not being able to have the life you really desire creates a spectral longing for another existence. A ghost life . . . running alongside the one being lived.' I think of all our ghost lives, shapeshifting this year, becoming moth-light.

Had then, of course, to google 'Fog' by Carl Sandburg: the wee cat feet; the 'silent haunches', oh my.
K has painted the most divine moons with paint she made herself. I am drawn to her, to the way she carves out her place as a feminine being in this world.
Proofs are in the world of *Those Born With Wings* – mine and Baz's collaboration. They will arrive with a feather. (I almost wrote wing; what a thought!)

Alone for the first time in over eight months. What a wild year.
Anna Jones' dhal, with edible flowers, in the soft afternoon light.

'Maybe this is your mission: to gather the bones of these girls, piece them together, give them a voice and then let them run, free and unfettered, wherever they have to go.'
Words from *Dead Girls*, Selva Almada, tr. Annie McDermott, sent by J, a woman I feel so close to, despite having yet to meet.

2nd

M and I met six years ago today. Our lives and our love feel, with every day that comes, as though they have always existed. As though they are only just beginning. Love is the thing, the only thing; it is our only hope.

S sent me, in the very early morning, words she sent another friend (also without babies) years ago, about writing and trying to keep fear at bay. It says something like – go and watch the birds, opening and closing their beaks – and honestly I did this just now, and I am more grateful for this grounding wisdom than I could ever really say. I need to remember this always, this afternoon spent worrying about things outwith my control, then calming my whole being down by simply watching the birds outside my window. It feels so important; as though all I need to carry with me into this next stage is held inside this simple act, somehow. I tried, as the afternoon unfolded, to hold this wisdom close. I lit the last beeswax candle, lay on the sofa and arranged all the pebbles into ascending size order. I let the silent world carry on around me – the dog in her bed, my love on the road, the birds at their work – and I allowed myself to shelter in it all. In the absence of the echoing. It felt, for the smallest of moments, as though no other reality could exist.

Then, outside the window, as if from nowhere and everywhere all at once; rain like the ending of days. Rain that neither added to the silence nor detracted, rain that kept in beat only with its own self, its own indubitable rhythm.

P has received TP in proof. I am terrified, sick to the stomach.

3rd
Two years ago today the very first proper sections of the essays that became the book were published. Time is so unbearably weird, as odd as two left feet, etc. We celebrated at Shoot the Crows in Sligo. I was a drinker, still, so full of much I no longer am full of. Is that girl gone? Is that good or bad – if so – is it either? Not shocking that I spent the afternoon imagining the sleeve of moths I promised myself if I made it

to a year sober. Nearly two, now; I am ready to mark this time on my aging skin.

Message in my inbox from the moon: DO YOUR BEST.

4th

Me and the dog are van girls again, thank goodness.

Never so glad to see a set of wheels in all my life.

Back to Derry. I am changed by this time away in ways I never knew could be real.

It is a different me that crossed the border & o, o, o this wild, beautiful life; full of grace & longing & unimaginable hope.

The River Foyle.

RIVER / DIVER / GIVER

Of myth & of broken things (& bringer of peace)

5th

Reviewed, for the *Irish Times*, *Antlers of Water*. Such an exquisite collection of writing; so full of hope. I needed, so badly, to read it.

Woke in J's home, which felt surreal; what a thing to be in the home of someone else.

Delivered sweet peas from our garden to her wonderful new shop.

Saw Dad for first time since Imbolc. Much too early to share the news, of course.

More tired than I thought humanly possible. In bed, now, at 9 o'clock.

7th

M has gone back to Correaly to do some work with M.

Met R for lunch, could have cried tears of joy just at seeing her smile.

It's been a woozy few days. Migraine the like of which I have never had and can't take any pain relief. Such severe morning sickness (in the evenings, laughably).

Before bed: GLIMMER.
Dusty-winged moon-beat.
(A mother of pearl.)

8th
Roseanne Watt's *Moder Dy* on the train.
Feel so overwhelmed I can't convey it, even.

9th
Have been looking at old pictures from living in Bristol.
Old lives, old maps, old beauty.
Is that part of my life gone for ever?
(Want to hide until it all feels better.)

10th
Katie Holten has drawn a flock of 138 curlew couples, dwindling down to a solitary bird to represent the record of breeding birds in Ireland last year. Signed the petition but at such a loss as to what else to do; what to do that might make a real difference.

Happy birthday Mary Oliver.
'I want to be light . . . beautiful and afraid of nothing, / as though I had wings.'

11th
Gwendolyn Brooks, as night falls, on green and on spring.

'To the Young Who Want to Die', oh my.
Swam, at lunchtime, with M before he left. He seemed to really
love Lough Owel.
We have floors now, thanks to him and M.

12th

M building us a kitchen.
I went down a rabbit hole on Instagram searching for all the
kitchens in which we have planned and cooked and quarrelled
and loved together. So many, so much cooking, so much loving.
Irish restrictions began half a year ago today. The only image
I have of that day is the sun going down.

13th

Reading, for the first time, the journals of Katherine Mansfield.
Could weep with the beauty of it, the fragile tenderness.
Didn't know tiredness like this existed.
An image, on Instagram of course, of a strikingly beautiful
older woman, in the mountains, carrying a vast burden of earth
on her head. Can't let go of the image, even to sleep. Carry
it with me in the afternoon as I try to rest. See her in many
of the places I have lived; the burdens I have carried.

[Seen & unseen fears
Collective grief, just beneath our own skin.
Placing the safety of others above our own desires.
Remaining silent just because it just aches too much to voice.
LOSS
LONELINESS
GRATITUDE for privilege.]

14th

Apples & Ash, Apples & Ash, Apples & Ash . . .

On Lit Hub, the most exquisite piece about Mansfield and the act of creating, left me echoey & spinning all day: 'When I pass the apple stalls I cannot help stopping and staring until I feel that I, myself, am changing into an apple, too — and that at any moment I may produce an apple, miraculously, out of my own being like the conjurer produces the egg. When you paint apples do you feel that your breasts and your knees become apples, too?' Words from a letter to a friend. Oh to feel the work in breasts and in knees, so bodily, so fully, so joyfully!

On a second read of Rebecca Tamas' haunting *Strangers*, and one of the seven butterflies currently in this small house landed on the word 'communicate'. Moments later, as I tweeted this, one of the house martins flew into the house. It is more than unbelievable; this life we share, this earth.

15th
Thinking of folk in America, breathing air that is hurting them every day. We won't be done 'til we wreck this place irrevocably, it seems. Our beautiful, aching earth.

Strandfield.
Lavender & shadows.
Baltray.
Swam beneath blue sky.
Felt like I began to become a mother today.
Unsure why.

16th
The sky is so full of majesty, today, the leaves so full of caterpillars.
Nancy Campbell's *Fifty Words for Snow* arrived. I devoured it

in a single sitting. Am moved by it so deeply, changed by it so utterly. We are learning to make peace with the thought of a long, isolated winter ahead, the last one of my life I will spend in this version of me. Her words have soothed my worried heart, my mind, my bones.

17th

Yet again, an image on Instagram leaves me taken aback and makes me think in a way I never would have before seeing it. This time, a beautiful illustration. A woman with a pie chart circle as her head, depicting feelings, mood and so on. Gorgeous watercolours and hand-drawn font show the biggest piece of the brain-pie is given over to WORRIED. Other slices include CONFUSED, DARK, SAD and so on, but there is, too, a slice allocated for GRATEFUL. I have never been more moved by a picture diagram in my life. My GRATEFUL would, today, be slightly bigger than WORRIED; tomorrow could be a whole different diagram. Each day so different from the next these days. I wonder what to blame on the pandemic, what on the pregnancy, what on the fact of simply being alive. No matter what, my TIRED would need its own circle.

Gathered a handful of love-in-a-mist from the garden and only realised I was crying when I went to find a vase beneath the sink. Thinking lots about the many hours given over to therapy; trying to find my own ways of coping – how I worry perhaps this time has undone much of the hard work. Feel, even on thinking this, both ridiculous and selfish in equal measure but still I can't shrug the worry off. Hormones, I am sure, or if not sure exactly – hopeful.

Instagram, yet again, delivers an image I carry with me the whole day through. A beautiful woman feeding wild swans, all

soft & yellow, all muted and ethereal, all light. I click through
to find its maker, only to find an advertisement for an online
mothers' circle next week. The opening lines: 'Wildflower
mothers work in the world of wonder and curiosity. They
know to trust the unknown and expect the unexpected.
They may have a destination but know to let go of how and
if they get there,' and I stop right there, too angry, too shaken,
to read another word. Clicking back there right now, mere
hours later, I'm unsure what unsettled me so, which of these
sentences left me so rattled; so ungraceful, so fucking peeved.
The image seems to grow more beautiful with each glance,
though, and I remember to check the artist, finally – Arthur
Joseph Gaskin – and wonder if his wild mother called him
Arty, ever, like H's delicious wee man. Gosh I miss them, and
Cornwall, so much. I google him, Arthur, and find the painting
is *The Wild Swans*, the woman is not a woman but a girl. The
swans are her brothers, and she is giving them the shirts that
will turn them human once more. It is the last painting before
he died, and all I can think of is his mother, the mother of
this fine artist – this man that used his hands to create such
beauty. This man whose hands grew inside the body of a
woman. A woman who kept him safe inside of her, for three
long seasons of her life.

Queasy queasy queasy. M made me egg in one of the cups H
made me, which felt so magical after thinking of her so much
this morning. I have a very good man, the very best man
indeed.

Found, before the sun set, sown by the birds, a tall bright
sunflower. Right where the barbed wire of the railway line
meets the garden. Just in front of it there are sweet peas so tall
as to almost reach the roof. Will never get over the fact that I
grew these. They were small seeds, and I placed them in the

ground, and tended them; attended to them as they grew, reaching for the sun. The wild-flower patch is more beautiful than anything that, before now, I have ever seen with my eyes. Will I ever visit Derek Jarman's Prospect Cottage? Will I weep there, if ever that day comes?

The swallows are almost all gone. Sat beside the rose wall, the dancing scent of them and the lavender all around, and watched the last of them zip around – on and off the telegraph line – on & off, off & on, like flashes of a light.

Fell down a Peggy Angus rabbit hole before bed. What inimitable gorgeousness. The design 'small medallions' is just so so good.
Taken, quite a lot in fact, by her name, too.

18th

Birds and light, each dancing on the wall, in the early light of morning.
Arrived in Derry to a perfectly blue sky.
Swam in the Swilly as the sun began to set. I cried in the water (of course I did).
Z read and said she loved the book. Such deep relief.

19th

Dunree with the wee moth in the first hours of morning.
She and I, straight into the body of the sea with our bodies.
Swimming with oystercatchers beneath the Urris Hills.
A joy to be with her again, her smile, her laughter, her joy.
Then a wander round the fort and hot chocolate outside.
How I have missed this, this ordinary unfolding of a day.

20th
Púca.

21st

Back with *Time Lived, Without Its Flow.*

'Instead of the old line of forward time . . . you live inside a great circle with no rim . . . I continue to sense daily life as paper-thin. As it is.'

From 6 p.m. tomorrow, restrictions in the North will be the strictest in the UK. I have no idea when we will see those we know again. Will it be autumn, or winter? Time feels changed beyond all comprehension, and we are changing with it, so used to being so alone.

'If you had once sensed the time of your child as quietly uncoiling inside your own, then when that child is cut away by its death, your doubled inner time is also "untimely ripped" . . . By what means are we ever to become re-attached to the world?' Denise Riley, oh my.

I am a howling mess even trying to imagine what she went through, even trying to imagine a way through such loss. Motherhood has already changed me, altered my sense of being in this world in ways I would never have believed before you were inside me.

Stay there, curled up – like all things in this universe that make spiralling curlicues out of their beings – for just as long as you should, as you need. Please don't leave me, before you have even arrived.

Please stay, please stay, please, STAY.

22nd
Cónacht Fómhair, Equinox

Harvested handfuls of poppy heads. Have begun to feel a little calmer than earlier, thankfully. I placed, for the first time, in

the soil – seeds – & waited in a way that I,
before, had never known how.
Light – unseen, unheard, unbelievable – came from cracks; in
the whole vast, quiet world
– & taught them how to dance inside the circle of becoming.

What a thing. What a year.
Last breaths of it, a chance to review our lives and ponder how
to spend the final weeks of the year 'til Samhain – balanced and
with intention. A moment to lean into the grounding that can
be found at this point of the circle, despite how different the
seasons feel this year. In ancient times, rituals were held at this
time to cleanse out the old energy and make space for the new.
A dance between light and darkness, life and death. A chance
to seek harmony, to clear space, to make room for the new – for
all we need to guide us through the darkness, for all that awaits
us in the coming winter. I realise, as the day slips away, how
much more deeply I have felt the shift this year and wonder
which of all the things I should hang that upon.

Swallows still about are slowly making ready to leave, following
their kin.
The door is open for winter.
Our bones are ready to loosen, to be transformed, to be
strengthened.

(I am ready too, despite the doubts. I am ready.)

23rd
lightlightlightlightlight

A sunrise to beat away the worries, to displace all the fears.
Woke beside my beautiful Sarah Gillespie moth and felt such

gratitude for my existence I actually cried. Pregnancy or pandemic or sheer and utter exhaustion? Who knows or cares?

Katie Holten and my conversation is up on Lit Hub. 'I think of time as circular. Tree time, growing out from the heartwood, in ever widening rings,' she said. Oh yes, indeed. Oh yes.

Went to Galway to replace the broken laptop. Came home, instead, with a beautiful old wooden beam M pulled out of a skip in the West End, carried through the city on his shoulder, and managed to get into the van. I love him so incredibly much.

24th
Swam as the warm sun set and the half-moon rose.
On the surface, afloat, a white feather.
I held it to the pink of the sky and considered the meaning of stillness.
Pitta, home-grown kale & rainbow chard, tomatoes and an egg.
These moments are such sustenance.

25th
Autumn.
Freshly baked bread & orange-coloured soup.
No signs of the sweet peas stopping, though, and of this I am much glad.
Last few months of the year, last few days of the month, last few moments of the light, last few swallows of the season.

26th
Instagram gave me, in the early morning, an image of M and me on a light-soaked street in Derry, way back when. We are shadows. M is kissing my head and I am holding two stalks of

hydrangea. Every day of life I fall deeper. How lucky we are. Then, out to the first frost.

'I wish you a kinder sea.'

(Emily Dickinson as the end of the year approaches like an old sailor.)

22 months sober. I am such a fan of double numbers. Gosh it's been the hardest part yet.

27th

Instagram is loving the shadow memories this week.

Today – a small bunch of roadside flowers, picked from the cracks in ruined buildings – in Porto two long years ago.

First car-boot sale in oh so long. Handknit woollen slippers from a gorgeous woman. We taught each other to say thank you in the language of our lands. It felt unimaginably good. So soft and bright. Also – a red beret that I know I will never ever wear. We sat out the front afterwards drinking coffee and holding hands, and all felt good, so very very good indeed.

I am the kind of tired I never could have imagined was real.

28th

Having such a weird time on social media just now.

'Did I, or did I not, detect a note of annoyance in your letter? a quick scratch?' Vita Sackville-West to Virginia Woolf, on this day almost a century ago. Yes, very much this sentiment online just now but it is likely only my hormones, ha! Want to stop feeling like I am riding the waves of anxiety. Might need a wee break.

A glorious roast for tea.

30th

THINGS TO CARRY INTO THE
DARKER PART OF THE YEAR:

feathers
Connemara
the moon
the words
first light of morning
moths at sunset
rest
planets & stars
silence (nearly)
pink dreams
the sea the sea the sea
flowers gathered from a small stretch of land
books
hope

Child Moon

I told myself for years – over a decade, in fact – that I was OK with not having a child.

That I had made peace with the fact I was not going to be a mother.

I told others, too: the friends that cared enough to give me space in which to talk about it all. I told those I both knew and did not, those that asked – repeatedly – if I had ever thought of having a baby. I told the handful of family members that still dip in and out of my life, on occasion. I told random strangers on train journeys with friends and their babies. I told an editor. I told an old neighbour more times than even I felt comfortable with. I told colleagues, parents of children I taught and adored, an old man in Leith who left me unable to wear my favourite brogues because he slathered them with sticky glue carelessly. I told flatmates, the mother of a flatmate with whom I didn't share a language, I told the person who sold tickets at the zoo. I am certain this list could run for longer – much longer – but I am tired of recalling it, to be honest. I am tired and am ready to find peace with the years that left me feeling confused, with the comments that made me feel like I was not enough, like I was wrong; unwomanly; unhuman for sharing a different truth than so many others. The fact that I realised, very early into a global pandemic, that I had changed my mind, that I realised I had been hiding parts of my own truth from my own self – a personal eclipse – does not take away at all from the view I held (or felt I had held) for so long. I don't even know if I could say I changed my mind. I don't even know if I could say that I decided to become a mother. The language around motherhood, babies, the whole foggy, limitless unknown – doesn't feel like it quite delivers.

There is something not right; something lacking, something amiss.

This is a thing I am still learning how to navigate, if I am honest. The fact that things are very rarely black and white, despite me having spent most of a lifetime growing up around that narrative. I wrote (I tried to write) for many years about it all. About the way that sometimes I felt like I had to justify the way I felt (or didn't feel) about motherhood. Not motherhood in general; only my own decision not to. The language around it all left me lost, seasick.

It centred so fully around lack, around loss, around the not having.

Black and white, black and white, black and white.

The reality is though that the move towards us trying for a baby was far from simple, a million miles from black and white. Now, in this the very first trimester – the bit where it feels like it should all make sense – even now, still – I feel at sea. I am joyful, ecstatic beyond words. I am over the silvery-grey moon. But these are not the only feelings at work inside me. There is far too much going on in there to even try to compartmentalise.

I am scared, so scared, about becoming a mother.
I don't know where to turn – in memory or in person – to find the way through.
What is a mother?
What do they look like?
What does this word mean?
It is, surely, a verb, is it not?

How will I know the how & when, the where & why.

Who will show me the what of this all?

The only part that doesn't leave me quivering is the *who*.
For there is only me and you, wee one.

I do not mean to detract in any way from your pappa, your
wondrous, supportive, funny dadda – the one who made me
want this – all of it, but (and I worry, even, about writing this)
ultimately there is only just me and you. I wonder, every single
day that passes, if it is my childhood that has left me feeling
this way, my experiences. If it is the fact that I have mostly
only known what it means to be raised by a woman alone,
with no one else in the picture for long enough to really
matter. Or if it is the fact that so many women I love raise, or
have raised, their children alone, either actually and completely,
or more or less – the other parent still there, in the picture
but faded, muted – drawn on too lightly to properly decipher.
Until a few years ago, the only stories I had ever heard of a
mother leaving her babies were from other worlds than this
one. The world of gods & monsters & floods & battles, etc. I
google 'mothers abandoning babies' but click out almost
immediately as it hurts my heart too much. A quick scan of
memory throws up Moses, Hansel & Gretel, Oedipus,
Romulus & Remus – but I don't have the attention span to
research the ins & outs of this group – to find out what
actually happened to their mothers. I remember, of course I
do, but I don't want to go there, you see. Then, as if she had
been lingering just below the surface: Medea. I am unsure
exactly where she fits in with the other mothers, so traumatic
is the story. I realise, straight away, that she did not in fact
abandon them, her babies. The abandonment in her story is
of a whole different nature entirely. She brings me right back
to the beginning, though . . . mother is a verb, as well as a
noun, and I feel at sea, a ship without a sail.

Where do I look to now?

I wonder, too, if the pandemic has contributed to this sense of aloneness in this new place – the landscape of my pregnant body. I read, over and over, that motherhood is a journey. And my first thoughts are about the fact that most journeys I have made in life I have made alone. Alone from the very first step. Alone when I moved & ate, swam & walked, slept & dreamed, woke & rose. There is no call for pity here, whatever. This aloneness was very much a chosen way. I find myself now, though, away from others without choosing that, so to speak. It sounds ridiculous, or perhaps romanticised, to say that time spent with M feels, so often, like time spent alone. We have reached that stage together where we do not need to act, to pretend, even to speak – there is no longer any awkwardness left in the interactions that make up our days – for which I am very glad. So here we are, alone every day, together. Seeing no one we either know or do not. And now here I am, on what could potentially be the most life-altering journey of my life, with someone else inside me every step of the way. Even if I ever hand this small being over into the hands of someone else, someone I love and trust, for however long I feel able – I will always be their mother. They will, in some ways, always be inside me. This is not just an airy-fairy statement; research proves the existence of a long-time cellular connection between mother and child. In the 1990s, scientists found the first clues that cells from babies could escape from the uterus to enter the mother's body. They named this new phenomenon 'fetal microchimerism' – after the chimera, a monster from Greek mythology. Mothers have likely held traces of the babies they grew inside them in a plethora of places within their bodies after birth for as long as mothers and babies have existed.

I suppose all of this is to say that, as the autumn unfolds, so too does my sense of the baby inside me as a gift as well as a call to action. We edge towards the winter, onwards into the darkness – and I am struck by the responsibility and the beauty of it all, in equal measure. This newly forming person, whose cells may already be taking up residence in my organs, where they might stay for anywhere up to decades. All the while the outside world continues to turn, chaotically, out of our control. I ask M to take a picture of me, as each week ends, in the same place, at varying times of day depending on the sun. Right where the light from outside gives itself over to this small cottage.

Here I am, right in front of a black & white moth,
right next to a shelf with a line of grey above its books.

Here I am, my face turning away, as autumn light
dances on a white wall.

Here I am, my hands over my growing belly,
my face looking like I never once have before.

Here I am,
here I am,
here I am.

Deireadh Fómhair, October

Hunter's Moon
Travel Moon
Dying Grass Moon
Drying Rice Moon
Sanguine Moon
Blood Moon
Migrating Moon
Moon of the Changing Season

'Memory, that library of the soul'
Tove Ditlevsen

In the early days of our relationship my lover and I had very little money and lots of people taking the very little of it we had from us. We lived, to begin with, together in a small terraced house in the Bogside in Derry. My partner was already living there when we got together and had been for a few years. It had been a wreck when he moved in, so he got the rent for a song, as they say, on the grounds that he himself would do any of the work needing done to make the place more habitable. I knew the house well, long before we got together, in fact. I'd been back living in Derry again, before we fell in love, for a short while, trying to make a life for myself in the place in which I'd been born. Trying to make a home in a place from which I had been fleeing, over and over and over, for as long as I could recall.

We had circled around each other, M and I, for a number of years before. Then, that year I lived in Derry, only just turned 30, and drinking myself into oblivion, we collided with each other head-first, full-on. The circumstances were as far from ideal as two people could really imagine. We made a bumper-car site of that year, crashing into each other; then retreating; reversing to the farthest point away from each other, then, crash; head on again. I have never been someone drawn to the chaos of love. I have always been someone who shies away from confrontation. I was given no choice with much of the confrontation that my early life was coloured by. As an adult I have mostly chosen the path most quiet. But with M things were different, to begin with. I couldn't seem to be gentle when first I fell in love – with him, with me, with our relationship. It took me longer than I care to admit to really trust that he was going to stay, and I took that fear out on him.

Don't get me wrong, I well understand this is a common response to trauma. Don't get me wrong; I well understand how lucky I am he stayed. How lucky we both are to have found this love; one that has weathered such uncertainty, still in such fine shape.

The people who owned our first rented home fell into difficulty and had to sell quickly. We moved into an even more expensive place but managed to, on occasion, Airbnb a room out to people drawn to the newly hip, phoenix-like city of Derry. It was the first time M and I got to really experience what it was like to host – having not quite managed to acquire a set of shared friends to have over for dinner, drinks, dancing, etc. – as of yet. In the short time we rented out that small room, I learned more about our relationship than I had in the entire time beforehand. To live in close proximity with another, a very particular kind of daily interaction is required, in my experience. We must enter, as fully as we can, into a world entirely of our own making, that world of 'you and me'. We are different, you see, when we are alone with the person who is our person, than how we are around others. M and I shared our home only for a few hours at a time with other people before renting that room out, and those hours were only with close family. Even then, when others were around, I understood that we were being different from when it was just us two. Opening our home up to strangers was such an incredibly impactful thing for me, one through which I learned things about myself I never could have learned, either when living in shared communal homes or when living alone with M. This is a somewhat tricky concept to try and explain but it feels important to note it, especially almost a year into living in a small home together into which no other people have really even set foot.

You see, there are parts of us – parts that we might never

really have calls to meet – until very specific, nuanced circumstances arise. When these circumstances arise within our safe
space – our home – the way in which the self chooses to
respond is quite unlike any other thing I have experienced. This
is, of course, speaking only to my own experience. And so we
watched each other skirt around the edges of new people, varied
and strange, as we cooked, ate, washed up, talked and (once or
twice) drank together. To do these things, over and over, with
people one has never before met, is a gift too hard to properly
understand, let alone explain. We were, only just, learning how
to be together even just us two. Then we had found ourselves
learning how to be together in the company of a stream of
strangers, sometimes for a single night, others for a week.
Sometimes we would not even share a sentence with the guest(s).
Others we would talk with until the wee small hours, heading
to bed only when we could hear, in the alleyway outside, the
fox making short work of the overfilled rubbish bags.

The thing I found most interesting about that experience is
the way my memory has responded to a period in which I
met, in quick succession and for varying amounts of time,
dozens upon dozens of strangers. I have forgotten almost every
single one of them. No matter their age or gender, where they
were from or how they chose to spend their days – the only
ones I have managed to lock into memory are those with
whom I shared deep, open dialogue.

For what is human memory anyway?
What is it, how does it work?

Is it, too – like time – a human construct in a way?
We make, through our own doing & undoing, the words &
images with which to create a story.

The stories we choose to remember are the ones that matter.

Memory is one of those things I seem to be drawn towards over and over again despite having very little working concrete knowledge about it whatsoever. Or perhaps this lack of understanding is precisely what calls me to it, siren-like, haunting. I first became obsessed with the concept when I was studying for my A levels. I remember learning titbits of information about memory – basic, memorable – in form class. They were trying, I remember, to teach us how best to ram our brains full of what we'd need to regurgitate in our exam halls – in order to gain the marks required to begin the rest of our lives. There was something about wearing the same perfume for each revision session, recording our notes to listen to whilst sleeping; choosing particular colours for underlining and highlighting in each specific topic, and other parts that have long faded from the tapestry that particular part of my life has become in my mind. It was a hideous time, a time I am glad to have (almost completely) managed to erase from my memory.

My dreams, the year I sat those exams, stopped completely and I was, for a vast period, convinced that they would never come back. That I had broken my brain through a combination of pulling too many all-nighters, not eating properly, anxiety and – most worryingly to me of all – fucking with my memory. Dreams are, are they not, a vital part of how we cognise our lived experience, through a complicated process that works with what has happened, how we dealt with it, and how we remember it all (or don't). I begin, almost immediately, to doubt myself; my understanding of this universal, dreaming world. I turn (where else?) to Google – 'What are dreams?' – and the very first return – Medical News Today – tells (reminds?) me

'Dreams are stories and images that our minds create while we sleep.'

What does it mean, then, when we can no longer find it in us to write these stories? To place, in orders both wild & ordinary, grotesque & glistening, these images from our lived experience. What, exactly, is going on inside a person when the dreaming mind stops working?

And what is going on in the opposite instance? When a person's dreaming mind, years after having vanished without a trace, arrives at the foot of the bed once more?

My dreams, since I began carrying a baby, have become so vivid, again, so real. They have become almost exactly like how they were before I started drinking, like how they were before the year I sat my A levels.

I try to unravel what this all might mean but find myself overwhelmed, exasperated, as bone-tired as weary knows how.

I have – on more occasions than I can count – dreamed about a man I have never met.

A man at a night-market in Australia.

A man who is selling his wares.

No, he is giving them away, it seems.

He will take no money for these things with which he wishes to part.

These things like a fabric snake made of remnants of a variety of old material – striped, floral, dotty, plain, faded. Things like tin soldiers that have lost – arms, a head, the tip of a gun, the left foot. Things like buttons & bottle tops, a broken metal toast-rack, a set of tissue flowers – shocking pink, clementine orange & faded lavender. Things like old cassettes that he cannot guarantee still play, a wool jumper – started but unfinished –

each sleeve left in a different, unusable state, various pieces of bone-handled cutlery like we used to have in primary school. Things like a wee yellow pocket-size guide to making shadows on the wall using only your hands. A more-than-half-used tin of chestnut-brown shoe polish six years out of date. A small felt mousey with only one black-beaded eye.

He will take no money for these things; instead he wanders around the concrete warehouse as four men in their late thirties with handlebar moustaches and (almost) matching tweed outerwear play a variety of circular stringed instruments; choosing (seemingly at random) the object he is going to offer the person he has approached, silently.

The man at the night-market was a very important part of the very important conversation I had with S – a woman whose friendship I will be grateful for always, that locked her into my memory, my mind and my life – when she came to stay in our small Airbnb room. She gave me him, you see, as a way in. She gave me him as a way to draw close to her, to try to know her; she gave me him as a way to make me feel safe in our interaction.

I don't know for quite some time – until I ask her and she writes to me – if this repeated dream is in fact me remembering a previous dream, or if the specificities are hodgepodge, garnered from books, films, real life experiences at real life markets and the like. I don't know if I've made the ins & outs of him up. If I have, in fact, *mixed* him up. But the thing is, when it comes to unknown characters – people we have never met and who might not in fact even exist in the physical world – does it matter? Can't I just allow them to put down roots in both these places; my dream life and the real world?

Must I always make it all so complicated, suck the joy away with my excavating ways?

From the moment I really began to think about it I became utterly, irrevocably obsessed.

I am talking about *memory*, of course.
I am consumed by it, of course.
I think about what it is, its role, what it means for our lives & our years – almost daily.

Why do we haul some things in from the deep blue of memory, let them remain in the net we stitched by hand, the one we have repaired – painstakingly – over and over through the years? Why keep a hold of the ones we do, when all the other memories are lost for ever to the salt and the foam? Why was the man at the night-market so important that I keep daily contact with the woman who gave me him, six years on, with almost 11,000 miles of land and sea between us?

I don't know if it is something to do with the algorithm, or if my phone has been listening in to my conversations before bed, but soon Instagram begins targeting me with posts about motherhood and traumatic memories. I am widening out my net. Maternal memory now has a tight grip – on my mind and on my phone – and I cannot reel it back in. Now my two great infatuations begin to dance together. I begin to think about time and how it plays out in pregnancy. I am only one trimester in but already I have begun to understand that all I thought I knew of time was wrong.
Suddenly I find myself doing it all so differently.
The measuring of, the marking of, the imagining of, the holding of – time.

NO, not all days are created equally. Nor all weeks, all months, all years.

NO, the hours do not add up the same way in all the days that we are given.

NO, the way it ticks & tocks, ebbs & flows, flies & drags & all of that – is simply not a given.

Is simply not a regimented, constant thing, to be held up to the light, taken as everyday, exemplary.

I am not living in the everyday, you see.

I am not living in the flow that I have long been fooled into believing is normal, real.

I am living in all the times (and all of their mirroring, their ripples, their trickster foolery) that I have ever before known.

Is there a distinctly maternal form of lived time?

How could there be anything but?

Will I experience time and memory – the elusive dance between the two – differently again – when (if) the wee one is born? Will either of the two go back to feeling how they did before my world changed shape entirely? I read everything I can about the science behind it all. The forgotten names, the sense of the nights stretching out, the days losing any sense of individuality and so on and so on, but even still it all blows my mind in ways I do not feel quite equipped for.

I read that a mother's brain in the forty days following delivery is nothing short of incredible. That the logical, rational, thinking part of her brain, the prefrontal cortex, goes offline – diverting her mental energy to the amygdala – the part of the brain responsible for emotions, empathy and nurturing. This process is often referred to by neuroscientists as 'synaptic pruning'. This is very similar to pruning a fruit tree. New neural pathways are being constantly created, helping the mother into her role as caregiver for this brand-new creature. These new brain connections are enabling the maternal brain to synchronise with the baby's brain. This is the process through which mothers learn to love and care for their newborn babies. Exposure to severe stress can disrupt adaptive changes in the maternal brain and impact maternal empathy. In effect, this forty days after birth – the fourth trimester – can impact on the mother and baby's brains for both their lifetimes.

(No pressure, then, of course.)

What does all of this do to the way a mother finds herself in the world?

1st

What did I dream last night? I dreamt I was the moon . . .
I was like that: visible invisible visible invisible.
There's no material as variable as moonlight.

Alice Oswald

What did I dream last night?
I dreamed I was carrying (once more) the antler – now hung above the bedroom door – found in the field at sunset on Mother's Day.
The day came back to me so intensely that when I woke, I felt almost scared that I was in our room confused by the power the mind has over us in sleep.
The colours. The feelings. The tears.

2nd

Reading, with the heaviest of hearts, Derek Mahon as the day begins:
'Everything is going to be all right.'
  EVERYTHING IS GOING TO BE ALL RIGHT
  EVERYTHING IS GOING TO BE ALL RIGHT
  EVERYTHING IS ALL RIGHT

3rd

Review of Rebecca Tamas' glorious *Strangers* up on Caught by the River. I think about some of her sentences almost daily.

4th

So many vast changes for us all on the horizon, certainly the case for me and M.
Pretty hard few weeks but never not grateful to the friends that reach out when I am terrified; that mind me through the darkest day. They are vital.

6th

Spent the morning thinking about the deep connections I have made this year with strong women. About why that matters so very much.

7th
light
hope
joy
strength
courage

(Every day as the light fades from the world outside, it takes up residence again, inside of us.)

8th

A beautiful, rhythmical sound, like the boats, when they rattle, in the winter winds.
Heard the heartbeat for the first time.
Saw, dancing on a screen, not the way they wanted them to dance at all, my first baby.
Safe, well, more real than I could ever find the words for.
I am undone and woven back together again.

11th

Dreamed, for most of the night, about the Foyle estuary. About the golden streaks through the grey. The egrets. The train line cutting through. The pink that only seems possible where the mouth meets the water – with Donegal straight across. Fuck it is all so much; too much, sometimes, to be alive.
Seems I am swimming my way, in any body of water that'll have me, through the wildest time imaginable. Every day is Mental Health Day and every day I'm grateful to those that

guide me through. (I was too gone to even think about it yesterday, etc.)

Perfect sliver of a moon in a pale blue sky. The moon, though. What a thing.
Rachel Cusk by a flaming stove seems the most autumn of all vibes tonight, for some reason.

13th
Last night, amidst the worst anxiety-induced meltdown I ever recall having (utter isolation, knowing no one, unimaginable personal change I never before dreamed of – during a global pandemic, being landlocked as someone for whom the sea has been the main source of healing, first book worries & so much other privileged BS) – we were dragged out to the ebony sky by the call of wintering geese, arriving in the starry sky. Our first time hearing them above our wee home. My lover, in that moment, holds my hand, tells me everything is going to be OK. That we are all going to be OK. That it is going to be OK. Above it all, the call of the geese, ignoring all borders, trusting in the strength of their own frost-tipped wings, despite it all.

14th
A white circle. A tin-glazed earthenware plate, found in a London sewer, reads, in exquisite blue ink: 'You and I are Earth, 1661', and never on this entire earth has there before been something so beautiful. I am utterly and unstoppably obsessed.

Hours upon grey morning hours given over to reading about Maude Delap. Her drawings, her records, her whales, her gender. So many words read and don't feel even an inch closer to her; try as I might. Oh, the Atlantic, the vast, untameable unknown

of it – and all us ones drawn into its secrets. Maude. Such a
gorgeous, singing name.

Afternoon spent writing about a dead goldfinch, a lost ash tree,
sowing seeds and a secret – then legging it for sunset in the
sycamore field.

15th

Katie Holten's tree alphabet, in Visual Carlow, spelling out
Heaney's words on wintering, left me bawling. I'm such a sap
when pregnant, more so than I even was before.
Van's broken, nowhere to go anyway, so I spent the day sorting
books for dark winter nights of reading and feeling fiercely
grateful. Even this year, with days that have felt heaviest of all,
there still are gaps for the light.
Thin Places, where miracles still might find a way.

16th

Ghosts of war, in all their hollowed-out hauntings.
(Reading about violence an awful lot this year, completely
unintentionally.)
For light relief, today, in one sitting (as always with her) – Annie
Ernaux's *A Man's Place*.
Bones rattled. Heart fluttery as a moth. She is all the things
that are good about the work.
Finished, way too late into the dark night, *On Being Blue*.
Enjoyed it but felt, continuously, as though parts of it were
missing, somehow.

17th

A striking image on Instagram from the Harvard College
Observatory archive. Black & white, and so achingly tender.
The new moon, in the arms of the old, as though cradled, as

though dancing. Oh fuck, it is the moon. It is always, always the moon.

'I begin to doubt beautiful words. How one longs sometimes to have done something in the world.'
   Woolf, as always, with her finger on all the pulses.

18th
Driving to get groceries with a somewhat fixed van, and I am in floods of tears listening to, of all people, Marcus Mumford – singing traditional ballads of a Sunday morning in autumn – and I suppose that is OK, now. That is more than OK, these days, I suppose.

Kettles Yard are showing three sketchbooks made in Alfred Wallis' final year, opening next week, and I am heartbroken knowing I won't go. Seems so incredibly silly but important to write the feeling down, I suppose. Went down a hole looking at the Tory Island painters, which left me even more distraught. Oh Donegal. Oh my.

Reading *Snow Country* by Yasunari Kawabata and am blown away entirely.

19th
Felt, for most of the day, a deep, unstoppable sadness. Then read Maggie Smith's 'First Fall' for the first time and I am changed for ever by her words. Oh wee one, I cannot wait to share this world with you; this glistening, gorgeous world!

20th
Why do we swim? Because it's the only way through the waves. Because it's who we are. We are the stuff of ancient seas. No matter how far we are from the shore, we keep swimming.

22nd
Back to the strictest of lockdowns with the kindest, funniest person I know.

Moon news: she is golden, she is dancing, she is still there
(she is the stuff of dreams & of the sea, she is the stuff of all that is seen & not)
she is beauty unrivalled.

24th
So much to be grateful for, so much cause for joy.
Back, for the however many millionth time, with Ann Gray's hen.
Doireann Ní Ghríofa, in conversation, on writing as an act of compulsion. Yes!

25th
Moonrise above the central bog of Ireland, on the first day of winter.
In the early morning, the woman on the radio said, when talking of the wintry weather and the darkness outside: 'We go on,' and it was utterly beautiful.
Words from Instagram: 'Shame dies when stories are told in safe spaces.'
And more, from beloved DJ: 'Blue is darkness made visible.'

26th
Water has always been its biggest secret, ebbing & flowing, an echoing silence

(the moon again, of course).

27th
Reading, in bed, about sound and babies in the womb.

The new Jeremy Cooper arrived so I have cancelled all of today's plans.

An early copy of TP is with B at Barton Books and he is reading it on the rocks at Penzance and my heart might break in fact.

15 weeks.

28th

Read, in all the hours I was awake yesterday, *Bolt from the Blue* and was floored by it. The raw emotion of it all, done so skillfully, so hauntingly.

Inside me this morning, a pear-sized, see-through creature is learning how to move its limbs.

It can hear, for the first time this week, my voice. My reading and singing. The sound of its athair calling to the dog in the field. The rain falling on the tin barn-roof.

It may sense, in the world outside the womb, light.

Eyes, a nose and ears are making their way to the places they will be for life.

This creature is forming inside me – another creature – unseen, unfelt as yet, growing like a soft, furry seed.

What a surreal, utterly beautiful world.

A glorious walk after the vet & doctor, then home to *Winter Papers* – a piece of work of which I am exceedingly proud.

30th

Woke up finally feeling somewhat human after a night of the worst sickness of second trimester. Reading Elske Rahill's *In White Ink*. Just WOW.

31st

Samhain storm.

Entering into the silken folds of the darker part of the year.
The circle turning, guiding us towards stillness.

Brón (1) Sorrow; (2) To grieve
Bronnlár, Exact centre

Stones & eggs,
bones & nests —
solid objects,
to be cradled in my hand,
to be weighed,
to be held up to the silent light
— *to be kept.*

A full year and a single day after I ended contact with someone I'd loved more than any other, who'd delivered unimaginable pain into my life, I opened the front door of my small stone cottage to find a dead goldfinch. The day after that one, I lay back on a hospital chair – masked, my belly covered in chemical gel – listening to the most beautiful, rhythmical sound I'd ever heard, like boats rattling against one another, in winter winds. It was a sound I'd spent a decade and a half being told I should never even hope to hear, due to complications brought about by another form of loss; a physical one my body had experienced during my twenties – the loss of cells. Cells that multiplied, that separated, that split into fragments. Cells that had to be cut out, lasered out. Cells I had no choice but to simply bleed out of my insides. Cells that left my body damaged, a changed map, a broken landscape. Cells that, through the very fact of their existence, had written a very particular life on my behalf. A life that I had, only just this year, begun to accept.

I dreamed – more than once it must be told – a goldfinch child. It told me, that dreamed bird child, over and over, night after night, that – despite the burning and the melting – the loss and all the grief – that there still was hope for this exquisite, dancing earth. Their presence in my nights, those months back then, felt such a gift, a way to make peace with their absence in my waking life.

I have found myself, in the middle of a global pandemic, as climate emergency ripples across our planet, carrying another human inside of my own self. I feel like I am held inside the thinnest place I have ever set foot. All that I once thought I knew of this world seems faded at the edges, replaced by a ghostly, dancing light.

The way in which it all happened hinges, as much of my life has, around ageless, inherited loss – passed from one generation to the next. A crow-black shroud of ache & suffering, borrowed trauma, anger red as blood. The knowledge that something so tender as the creation of new life can arrive in our lives on the tailwinds of such inconceivable loss, has done something to my insides. It has cleared a space, just as one might sweep out the ashes from the previous night, before criss-crossing freshly gathered kindling in the heart of the hearth. I too feel that something has been carried out of me – from my centre – to make room for a fire that I never thought that I could build. This newly created space is quiet, bordering on silent.

Autumn has come, taken away the leaves from the trees, set its winds rattling at our teeth and our home like the cailleach. The light has begun to drip out of the sky earlier, and earlier. I stand at the doorstep and watch it leave the day behind. I read, as night falls on a grey day, about indigo buntings. Aimee Nezhukumatathil tells me: 'There is no other blue like the blue of these birds . . . They navigate by following the North Star . . . know [it] by heart, learn to look for it in their first summer of life . . . how they must have spent hours gazing at the star during those nestling nights, peeking out from under their mother. What shines so strong holds them steady.'

I begin to wonder what light my wee bird will be drawn to if they come. To wonder what I can do to keep them safe on nestling nights, as this world turns and burns and glows. What light can I point them towards? What light can *I* find, amid this all? I only know pregnancy as another part of an already surreal, confusing year. Will any part of it feel normal in the months to come?

Will the wee one be OK?

Will I?

Will we all?

As the autumn begins to unravel,
I find myself apprenticed to observation.

I take to reading books about the weather.
I take to paying attention to the light.
I take to writing you letters about the world
outside our window.

This world I cannot wait for you to see.

Samhain, November

Frost Moon
Beaver Moon
Trading Moon
Digging Moon
Snow Moon
Freezing Moon
Mourning Moon
Deer Rutting Moon
Moon of the Falling Leaves

1st
Stove on, candles lit, reading my first book to my first baby, on the first day of November.
Bothy pie for dinner.

2nd
On a train for the first time in so long. The moon hung above Lough Owel, the sky pinky-grey, full of starlings, full of grace.

3rd
A rainbow, above the canal, between showers.
Katie Holten's tree words about voting have moved me so, so much.
Indeed: the most radical thing we can do.

4th
Rusty-red hydrangea, in the sun, against a cracked white wall.
Oh Dublin, Oh winter, Oh life.

5th
Finished audio book.
Bought blue hydrangea from a woman who should not have been trading but was.
Train cancelled due to pandemic. Bawled like a wain at the barrier with exhaustion, overwhelm, everything? The guard bought me a Kit Kat and honestly, it was one of the most touching gestures of my entire life. We are still human, we are still capable of the most simple, loving goodness.

Need so much silence now, so much silence for an extended period of time.
14 weeks.

6th

So hard to get out of bed today. The Unthanks and the birds outside the window by my desk helped. Am I falling into the dark again, or am I just tired and full of hormones and full of winter?

The light out there today is a kind I thought had long gone away. Thinking of Lorde, her grace, her wisdom.
'The quality of light by which we scrutinize our lives has direct bearing . . . upon the changes which we hope to bring about through those lives.'

7th

Nick Hand shared the most arrestingly beautiful image on Instagram, from a tree in Henleaze –
a swift – black thread embroidered on a simple cream square – with the following words:
THE SWIFTS WILL BE BACK.
I long to be the kind of person who can deliver such solace with only one sentence, anonymously.
A butterfly, woken from slumber, by a change in the world's winds across the water. Sometimes it is fucking exquisite to be living in these days that are the making of history.

8th

Rereading Berger's *The Red Tenda of Bologna* after reading Octavia Bright's piece on her father today. Such tender, penetrating words in both. Berger's lists, and how he sculpts time, oh my; 'Time will tell, he used to say, and he said this in such a way that I assumed time would tell what we'd both be finally glad to hear.'

9th

Just one more season left us two. When the spring comes, another wee soul will share this tiny space with us.

Totally unplanned, I shared the news of bábóg in person to someone for the first time after chancing upon MM at the lake. A new friend, one I only met once before, whose home I was in the day MD died. He already means so much to me, as does that lake. It was sheer chance we both were there given we aren't allowed to meet. When I told him there were tears in both our eyes. On the way home, we switched on the radio to chance upon that friend once more, talking about words for water. Oh my.

Tonight I'll sleep alone in the cottage, the first time either of us has done so.

10th

My first drinking dream for quite a while last night (because I'm writing about it? Because I was home alone?). In the dream I was pregnant whilst drinking. Woke up this morning to find – not a bottle of red wine on the floor beside the bed – but a trusty, snoring hound. What a wild thing the mind is.

MM's chard, L's dukkah and an egg fried by my lover. It is in moments such as these we find the way through.

My first Zoom meeting, many months after it became the norm, for *Winter Papers*. How odd but how wondrous to see the faces of others, if even on a screen.

Sat at a table made for me by the man I love, watching the birds he calls down from the trees with seed. What a thing it is to be alive, and to love.

11th
11.11, 20.20
Powerful portal, no?
The rain, the winds, and the robin outside my window, above the dog's snoring.
Then the first mince-pie of the season, to welcome my lover home.
Rereading *The Pity* after Roseanne Watt shared on Instagram; 'Making love to heal, making love to heal'; of course, of course, of course.

12th
Early winter light.
That is all, and everything.

13th
Collected, in the stillness of the near gloaming, what I think could be the last of the flowers. Poppy heads & exquisite, skeletal remains of love-in-a-mist, blue cornflowers fading into lilac, clover, & lavender from three different plants, sculpted quaking grasses & bright yellow fennel.
Grown, from seed, in my first garden.

14th
Ali Miller's words – 'Here I am now, with the accident of self' – feel like everything today.

15th
The first flutter. I am for ever changed.

17th
Anna Jones' Celebration Pie for dinner. Where does any of us begin with what we still have to celebrate, even now?

Mending my favourite grey jumper. Feels like an exceptionally important thing to be doing in these days.
Water births are now banned in Ireland. A deeply unsettling time to be carrying a baby here.

20th
First gift arrived for the wee one, a rainbow woollen cardigan, from RSJ, made by his mamma. She was born in Derry, making it all the more moving. Feeling so grateful for such gestures, here alone at this time but for M.
Just us two here, at this time of quickening.

21st
Wee one flutters as the first light arrives.

22nd
M made me an exquisite wooden frame for our piece by Jo. Now we go to sleep and waken with constellations above us.

23rd
Spent last night and all of today mending the silk jacket I got in a Stoke Newington charity shop but haven't been able to wear for years. Have told myself, for longer than I care to remember, that that is not the kind of thing I can do. I am quite moved by this for some reason (always with the being moved, these days, it seems). Making something more beautiful, despite its flaws, simply by giving it time and care, feels so good.

Alice Coltrane on the John Kelly show. The bábóg loves it. Proper wing-beat on my insides. Delighted to be halfway through growing a wain with such great taste in music.

24th

Two years sober.

Lay in bed watching light drip into the garden from a frosty, starry sky.

Wee creature inside flutters like a moth-bird against the window of my skin.

Should bring in the last of the kale and have with eggs.

The Blue Nile on repeat.

Howled like a baby beneath the sycamore, in gratitude.

26th

My baby is fluttering to This Is the Kit and I am so close to crying.

27th

Halfway grown round.

Moon above the garden, white, and mirroring.
Oak / Frost / Digging / Beaver / Mourning / Reed / Snow.
Light spills out from everywhere.

29th

First Sunday of Advent.

Got the tree.

30th

Mourning Moon.

Moon of the Oak, of the Snow, the Fog.

'The moon has nothing to be sad about
Staring from her hood of bone.'
Sylvia Plath

I've been into the moon for as long as I can remember.

This year, perhaps due to the fact of being in the same place for every full moon so far, I've begun to really properly consider it. That is to say: this year, my obsession with a large white rock has grown deeper, wilder. This year my desire has sprouted limbs. Now the moon is more than just a face, for me. Now the moon is all appendage, all movement. All sweet, haphazard crawling across the wooden floor of the sky. I see a meme on Instagram, about someone sitting in a college class, and the lecturer is talking to the students about calendars. The lecturer shares an image, saying something along the lines of: 'This is widely held as man's first attempt at a calendar.' The students are busy scrawling her words down, when she asks them a question (why am I so moved by questions, these days?): 'What man needs to mark 28 days? I would ask you if, perhaps, this is *woman's* first attempt at a calendar?'

I lose it, the meme – scroll backwards though I might I cannot find my way back through the small screen's vast laby-rinth. No matter how fiercely I swipe, with how much force, my finger can't take me back in time to screenshot the words I have been so affected by. Luckily, a basic Google search carries me back there, like a babe in arms.

It was a bone, of course.

(This year, it is always a bone.)

It was quite a well-known bone, although unknown to me before that meme.

The bone is the Ishango bone, discovered at the Fisherman Settlement of Ishango in the Democratic Republic of Congo. The bone is curved and brown. The bone has been carved, scraped, polished and engraved – too much to tell what animal the bone belonged to. An American mathematician, Claudia Zaslavsky, is the person that suggested that the creator of this bone tool may have been a woman. She suggested that the creator used this bone to mark lunar phases, in relation to the menstrual cycle. I am drawn in by the bone. I am drawn in by the mathematician. I google her, of course, to find she is an incredibly inspiring, empathic human being. An obituary written by her friend leaves me bawling, so tender are the words offered about the life and ways of this woman. I had hoped, this year, to find ways to write about time that were free of sentiment. Ways that were much more universal than how I often seem to communicate things. But the reality is that time simply won't let me. I am bombarded at every angle with tales of beauty & hope & pure, unrivalled goodness. I am left back where I started, a place I hoped to steer clear of. I am left all weepy and sappy, overcome by the feeling that there is nothing more exquisite and meaningful on this earth than the way we choose to spend our days. I am unable to be removed or neutral when it comes to talking about time. I think of what time means when it is lived in an altered state. During pregnancy, when grieving, through illness. At any moment we are held in a place or rhythm outwith our normal experience. I think of the things I have been taught about time, about mythology, creation myths, the idea of a cycle that will never end. Recently I've begun to wonder if we can even accept any of these as given any more. Recently I've begun to think of time as a curious creature, like the one growing inside me, that I might spend a lifetime trying to understand.

A Handful of Memories

I am sitting at a desk in the library at Trinity – looking at a small, enclosed office-cum-staffroom – covered wall to wall in ornamental owls. I am in my first year at university – in my first term – and I am wearing a long grey woollen coat purchased for a pound in the St Vincent de Paul charity shop in Derry. Outside it is raining on the cold, busy Dublin streets. A man is sitting in the space, feet up on the wooden counter that faces the desk, talking to a woman through the open counter window. He is bald and wearing black Doc Martens. I am reading, for the very first time, about Khronos – the Ancient Greek god of time. I read about how he castrated his father – Ouranos, Sky. I read how he swallowed his children as they were born: childless Father Time. I begin to understand time as something I will be drawn to, always, on this wet Dublin day.

The owls are in the memory as a collective. As things knit together that cannot really be separated from one another. Sometimes I try to convince myself that some were made of shells, say (the kind of thing found in old gift shops in Victorian British seaside resorts), that some were porcelain-white with blue flowers on their wings, that some were holographic (silver from one angle, purple, blue or green from another) but the truth of it is that I am making these parts of the memory up. There was, simply, a small room in a university library that was full to the brim with owls. A parliament of them, as I read, for the very first time, some of the very oldest stories written about the very oldest man of time.

My brother and I are on a beach, I think it is Downhill Strand
– a glorious stretch of golden sand on the north-west coast of
Ireland – directly below a crumbling, centuries-old library. The
library is in fact a temple, which is in fact a circle, perched on
cliffs which have been giving themselves back to the Atlantic
Ocean for a considerable period of time. I am four or five, I
think, because my younger brother is toddling in the memory,
quickly and forcefully but without great precision. We are on
rocks, watching as the water makes its way in towards the
dunes, towards the library that no longer has any books, perched
just above us and the cave that the train goes through on the
way here. Sand has collected in a wee hollow on the rock, a
space that, when the water comes in fully, will disappear. When
things go away, for my brother and I in the moment, they go
for ever. We are not yet able to understand the tides; the ebb
and flow; the flux of existence that allows this rock to be a
climbing frame at lunchtime today but that hides it away, only
for a few hours, then – for an hour at most – allows the hollow
to become a rock pool. Then, at long last, order is restored and
– if we came back – we could sit and have our sandwiches
on it again. Once gone from our view, a thing is gone for
good. It is what we know of the world, it is the way we accept
things so fully out of our control. It is the way we make peace
with the chaos that comes with being a small person in this
vast, ever-changing world.

We do not yet understand – magic tricks, sarcasm, algebra,
how to work the Ceefax. We do understand – that the stars
we watch as we drive home in the dark back seat, over the
mountain, past the Christmas tree forests – are not there any
more. They are gone, those stars. The light they are throwing
down to guide us home is like a photograph, like Santa, like
our granny's God. The stars aren't just far away, they aren't even
there at all, in fact. That we can see them now, when one of
us wakens in the back seat of the car with *Lovers Around 11* on

Radio Q102, is a trick that time plays to help us understand something else; something we aren't quite certain of yet. We do not understand, neither my brother nor I, a single thing about time.

On that beach that day my brother kicks all the sand out of the rock's hollow belly. Someone who is with us, an adult who isn't one of our parents or grandparents, tells us both off when he does this. The adult whose face, voice and identity have left the memory, tells us that everything is in its place for a reason we could never understand. They ask us, this faceless stranger, how we will feel if someone comes along, trips and falls into the rock – cutting themselves because we have taken away the sand that was supposed to protect them. My brother cries, I think, or maybe it is me. Either way no one falls on the beach the whole time we are there. The only tears shed are those of whichever one of us cried when this stranger that we must have known asked us that question – one I think about, still – more than three decades later.

I am slightly older than the day on the beach. My brother and I are with our father in St Columb's Park after school. I am wearing a blue coat with a dark green tartan collar. It is cold but not raining. I can't remember what my brother is wearing but pictures taken in and around this time, also in the park but not on this day, show him in a mustard coat with a hood so that might be what he was wearing that day, too. He is scowling in those photographs but not in this memory. We are climbing a huge tree. I want to say it is an oak, knowing the woodland in the park to be one of the oldest ancient oak woodlands in Ireland, but it would be me doing what I did with the owls. I haven't a breeze what the tree is, except to say that I know it is one my father took us to often, in rain & sun, in snow & wind. I said that we are climbing the tree but the reality is of course that we are sitting, safely, on a low branch, tucked in close to its ancient, knotted body. It doesn't matter – then or now – that I can't identify the tree. This tree is the tree I measure all others by and have done since long before that particular day, making it the tree of life, for me, the tree of memory, the tree that all other trees grew from.

This tree is the tree of time.

This is the tree I think of when you whisper 'tree' to me as I sleep.

My father has been exceptionally quiet until this point in the memory. He has not asked what we learned that day, what we had for lunch, if we have any homework. We have walked – the whole way along the Limavady Road, past the army barracks with only my brother and I babbling away to one another. Then, all out of nowhere, our father starts to talk to us in grown-up words. Like in the memory above, the words take the form of a question. Like in the memory above, it is one neither my wee brother nor I had any means to understand, let alone answer, so we don't.

'*Have you ever thought that maybe we aren't really real at all, just the dream of a sleeping tree?*'

My partner comes back from his first time away from the cottage since we moved in, our first time apart in almost a year, and tells me – without being asked – what he dreamed the final night he spent alone.

'I was driving down a lane, much like ours but not ours, and I had with me – in the passenger seat – my goat.' (My partner does not keep goats, nor any other livestock.)

'We stopped at a passing place to let another car go by, and my goat jumped out into the thick, dark muck. I got out to wash her off, immersing her deep into a seemingly bottomless puddle. When I took her back out, so much time had passed that I held in my hands, not my goat at all, but a huge black and white badger.'

Every time I think about time, I think of Margaret Atwood.

As a teenager I read everything I could get my hands on that she had written after reading *The Handmaid's Tale*. I remember feeling like it was only through encountering her work that I really understood what it meant to be a woman in a world so shaped by the violence of men. Encountering the violence itself, over and over, seemed not quite real, somehow. Reading about it, studying it – writing thousands of words and erasing them, cutting them up, sticking them all back together – made the violence that men inflict every day seem more real to me, somehow. That we live in a world the edges of which are held in place by the violence of men, sinks in for me over and over, through the words of other women.

I think of Atwood when I think of time in a very specific way.

I think of her holding a plastic, spiral-shaped pale pink straw in a glass of red lemonade, lifted out of a crate of an open-backed van. The straw is a little like the helter-skelter slide outside Barry's Amusement Park in the Victorian seaside resort I lived in for the first years of life except the slide was yellow. I have never tried to get this straw image out of my mind but even if I did I imagine I would struggle, so imprinted is it. Did Atwood write of time as a straw? More specifically, was this straw, if she wrote such a straw, the way I hold this straw in my memory? I likely do not need to tell you that I googled to see if I had dreamed or made this up, to find she – only just this month – wrote about the passing of time for the *Guardian*. It's a piece about a poem, and the place and time in which it was written. But it also is about grief – personal, collective, historical. To mark the passing of any time is to hang the things that have happened on a long clothes-line and watch as the wind and rain and all the other elements make short work of them. To mark the passing of time is to place all the things that didn't happen, all your hopes & dreams, your ache & longing, in the snow. To lay them down in the order you would choose, to give them over to the winter light; their surfaces suffused with peachy hues – and wait for them to be buried, for them to begin – slowly but with force – to be returned to the earth from which they came.

All the internet throws me back is a book she wrote that seems to be made out of straw. I remove 'straw' from my search, trawling instead for quotes simply about time, and find – 'Time is not a line but a dimension, like the dimensions of space' – from *Cat's Eye*. Did I draw the straw from this line about time not being a line?

Someone I care deeply for, though have met only once, sends me a book about lines. I am writing about circles, I think, until I read – over and over – about this straightened, ancient form. I am writing about how things begin without beginning, end without ever stopping. How everything we think we know is really a cavort between unseen ghosts and their shadows. I am carrying a circle in my belly that started as a line, as a seed, as the delicate dance between these two states of being. I am carrying the world inside me (but of course already I know this creature is the whole world curled into a small snail, waiting to unfurl).

I have to pretend (somehow) that there are other lines, other circles. That the small, dancing creature I have watched on a screen is not the only one in the world. Somehow, I must, when they come, go on living and breathing and working and sleeping as though anything other than the shape of their face matters. As though there are sounds other than the ones they will make; faces other than those they will pull. As though the world is the same world that existed before they arrived. I feel, at times, as though I could be quite good at this pretence. I convince myself I will travel — when we are able to — all alone, despite their arrival. That I will run and swim and tend to my wildness as though all is still the same as it was before. I tell myself, and others, that I will return to work as soon as they arrive; that nothing whatsoever will be different. That the writing will look and sound and feel and smell the same. I promise myself this as I sing to a small thing that has made a temporary home of my womb. I tell myself this as I am tucked up in bed — my head as sore as ever I have known — with no pain relief, trying to sleep on my side; trying to rock myself as I imagine I will the thing inside me, in a short while. I have these conversations with myself as I swim, as close to the shore as I can whilst still having enough depth. As I stay clear of the places, people and things that have, suddenly, begun to unsettle me too much to be around.

I am telling myself lies, and I know it.

I am giving in to the process we have only, in very recent years, begun to talk of. I am pretending I can be separate from it all. I am imagining that I am only a vessel allowing safe passage, that once the cargo is out, I will refuel, turn, and leave the harbour.

I do not want any of this, is the truth of it all. I do not want to carry on as normal when they arrive.

I want to be changed, I want to change, I want to be unrecognisable.

I want to be moved, I want to move, I want to be untethered.

(There is something in me that knows I have no choice, either way.)

I try to return to the lines, to the tenses as they should be, to the order of things that once I took as given but I can't. I read a book many moons ago about 17 near-death experiences a woman I knew had encountered (had survived) and the title lodged itself inside me like a splinter from a wooden floor: *I Am, I Am, I Am.* It used to be the kind of thing that left me red with shame, the fact I didn't know that the title, like that of the book you now are reading, is a line written by another writer, another woman. I had only read sections of Sylvia Plath's incredible, haunting work before coming to Maggie O'Farrell's equally moving memoir, and like I said, things like this used to fill me with such a sense of deep embarrassment. When I recall that version of myself, now, I struggle to comprehend why. Shame is a funny old thing to come to grips with, and I wonder if I will always be bogged down by it in one or other guise. Anyhow, the thing is that now, when I haven't read, seen or heard of something, I no longer try to make excuses. It seems such a small thing, but it makes a marked difference to my interaction with the work of others. I am learning, trying always to learn, trying to listen and in doing so to learn humility.

All this to say that O'Farrell and Plath's use of that phrase moved me, moves me still. What is it, exactly, that *I am* right now? And is that something, that someone, different from before? Will it change when you arrive, wee one? How could it not? There has been a tendency, in recent years, to criticise the use of the 'I' in works of non-fiction but there is nothing I want more, no matter what it is I read, than the 'I'.

I want to know about you.

I want to know all the 'I's there are to know, including my own.

The critic Alvarez said of the poems in *Ariel*: 'In a curious way, the poems read as though they were written posthumously,' and I want to scream from the top of the tallest building I can find – that cowshed with its rattling roof and its winter crows – that surely this is the case with *all* writing. With all words. With every single thought that leaves our insides to take its place in the world outwith our bodies. To write is to take the idea of time and smash it into millions upon millions of minuscule pieces. It is to hold a baby up in front of a mirror and watch as they forget, over & over, the narrative we have so readily invented about the self as being separate from the world. Of the self as being stand-alone and removed. We are each other, of course. Our 'I' is our own but every other 'I' too, somehow. The baby in the mirror is the baby in front of the mirror, is another baby, is every baby, everywhere. This moment is all of its own making, its own being. But it is, too, every other moment that has been, every moment that still will come.

How can any of us be expected to believe in time any more?

Will this moment we are living through ever end?

What was I thinking to try for a baby with the world in such a state?

What will it all look like when you arrive?

Am I ready for this, for you?

Can I even claim this role, *mother*, with all these worries at swim inside me?

What if you don't arrive?

What if I lose you before I even have you?

Truth be told, I had always thought I knew Plath's poetry much better than I actually did.

My closest friend, as well as being a beautiful mother, an incredible baker, an inspiring writer, is a doula. The name she has chosen for this side of her work is 'Morning Song', after a Plath poem.

Truth be told, I knew this poem was about mothering & babies and so I have, for many years, steered clear of it. Even this far into pregnancy there is a part of me that cannot; will not; believe I am becoming a mother (am I one already?). I lie curled up on the bed devouring my friend's Instagram doula posts as though they were the clementines I ate like they were going out of fashion in the first trimester. I scroll backwards in time from the most recent post.

Here she is explaining the newborn's need for closeness. Here is postpartum massage. Here we have the conscious breath, the need for nourishing food. Here are words on the loneliness of motherhood – until finally – here we are given the inspiration behind the name. Plath's poem, on the small, blue-lit screen in my right hand, typed out in full by the mother I love best in the world. It may not be of any surprise that I weep at the line that speaks of moths and roses; a far-away sea.

I write all the words of this poem into the notebook I have chosen to bring with me to hospital. I promise myself that these will be the first words written by another person that I will read to my child, as though I am trying to atone for something. As though already I owe the creature in my womb something (everything?). I am trying to make up for something, always, it seems. I cannot loosen myself from this sense of responsibility that hangs around my neck, for things I don't even know if I understand.

Cleitearnach, Flutter

And then, as the second part of the year begins to unfurl, you start to move.
Slowly, softly.
You are a moth-bird – beating your see-through skinned bones – against the surface of my skin.

At first, I am sure I have imagined it.
A shimmery dream of a thing, a silky ripple of some phantom pebble – unthrown – unreal.
To begin with I convince myself that it is wind, not outside, of course, but inside.
Inside the belly that now we share between the two of us.
But it is not wind, of course: it is *you*.

Newly formed, freshly made, you are learning how to move, inside the hollow of my curves.
It is *you*, of course.
Wee creature that one day, further along this unknown line – I will hold in ways so different from how I hold you now.
Tiny, fluttering thing – unseen, unheard – simply *felt*, in the parts of me I had never even known before you came.
The world outside my womb is full of counting.
Deaths and figures, tolls and losses.

I had to find a way to mark the days before *you* came, in a way that might feel different from all of that.
I had to learn, despite it all; to carve a space for hope.

I had to learn, despite it all; to carve a space for *you*.

Nollaig, December

Cold Moon
Oak Moon
Hoar Frost Moon
Little Spirit Moon
Long Night Moon
Drift Clearing Moon
Frost Exploding Trees Moon
Moon When the Deer Shed Their Antlers
Moon Before Yule
Moon of the Popping Trees
Winter Maker Moon
Midwinter Moon

'We talk so much of light, please
let me speak on behalf
of the good dark. Let us
talk more of how dark
the beginning of a day is.'

Maggie Smith

The only winter you spend inside me,
we are held within 5 kilometres of our stone home.

I had thought it might be different by now.

When we talked of you – trying with all our might not to
tend too tenderly to hope, keeping our words casual, carefree
– we counted forwards on our fingers and found ourselves in
a different year from this sad, confusing one. We saw the world
back to 'normal'. We saw lights back on; doors open; people
sitting together and going places. We placed our hope on the
bigger picture instead of the small and we were wrong. We
told the small handful of people we felt close to that you were
inside me on a shaky WhatsApp call. In one instance we did
not know if the silence was a signal delay or shock, or both
or neither. I attended every appointment alone. Your dadda
never saw you move on a screen or heard your heartbeat in
those early days. He still hasn't. Yet again, instead of trying to
leave space for hope inside me I do the opposite. I am shocked
by how easily I push hope aside. How good I am at giving up
my desire for experiences and moments. Do others find it this
easy? Does your father find me cold? Does he think I ought
to fight more when I'm there? To argue the case for his hand
in mine, his eyes on the screen as you refuse to move exactly
which way they want you to? The truth is I know that none
of this – these decisions made about you and me – about our
bodies – is within my power to control. If one thing is clear
to me, since we moved south of that unseen border, it is that
women and their babies still have a lot to suffer at the hands
of the state. The pandemic has merely made this fact more
visible, has only lifted the reality already there and held it a
little higher, a little easier for us all to see.

People talk of the 'new normal' and I want to scream. I am
too tired, too weary, even now, to try to unpiece why. The

vulgarity of the assumption that what came before was 'normal' unsettles me in a host of ways. The misconception that there was, before now, an idealised sense of the everyday. One which I feel sure simply could not have existed for so many of us. For a whole host of people who spent their days just trying to get through. Writing about it all makes me cringe. From early in, I have felt things to now be changed beyond compare, beyond any point at which we could go 'back'. As though time were some mark on the wall. Some X on a map drawn by people that have never even set foot in the place. I try, every day, every week, every month – as the seasons continue to unfurl – to strike a balance. I need to keep on caring, not to allow myself to become immune to the news that comes at us every day. But I need, too, to do my best to remain grounded, calm, hopeful. This wee one, and M, need me to be OK. I need that, too, of course. I remind myself every chance I get that it will be OK, everything will be OK, and that we are enough for the baby. That the baby will be OK despite what the past holds. The uncertainty of the future.

One day we wake up to snow that I had no idea was coming.

Where I come from, we can supposedly smell the snow long before it arrives.

We can feel it, deep down inside of us, nestled in beside our unseen organs.

Ghost-songs.
Memory-lines.

Before the snow, I gather – from a garden full of wren-song
and salmon-pink light – poppy heads. Grown from seed, in
the same summer that you began to grow. A handful of hours
later, I watch, from our bedroom window, whiteness hide the
garden away from view.

I hold my belly and I tell you,
for the first time,
of the place where I was born.

Of the place where I learned that nothing stays the same for
the whole livelong day.

That time ebbs & flows like a body of water,
that moments wax and wane like a milk-white moon.

I tell you of the place I learned
that nothing
precious is ever fully *lost*.

That nothing
beautiful can ever really
be *broken*.

I open our yellow door with its fox knocker – bought before
the world changed shape entirely – and I stand beneath a sky
that still feels full of magic.

Beneath a kind of light that takes the world and makes it
sing.

I stand in the garden listening to the song of new-born
snow-light.

And as you move, I realise you must hear it too.

Deep down inside of you, in beside my bones.

Talking of foxes, a woman I have not yet met tells me that her hen is giving away its secrets to the fox.

She is singing them, in fact, this hen.
  She is singing her secrets.
  She is singing the red fox a song of her babies,
  a song of her eggs.
  I send her, this woman I have yet to meet, a WhatsApp message with the following line – words I love more than I quite know how to say:

'I sing to my blue hen . . . / I tell her there is no present time / . . . a zebra finch can / dream its song . . . / I tell her how the Mayan midwife sings each child / into its own safe song. Tonight, the moon holds back / the dark . . . She makes a bubbling sound, / her song of eggs and feathers . . .'

The lines are from a poem by Ann Gray, that I have read over and over since I was first introduced to it through Cerys Matthews' Sunday morning show on BBC 6 Music. The first time I heard them, these dancing, aching words, I was in the attic room of a cold rented flat within Derry's city walls. I was so depressed I did not quite understand how I was still able to do things, anything. I did not, for the life of me, understand how a body could continue to keep on when its owner was in such a state of helplessness, of hopelessness – when its owner was in such a state of nothingness. This is what depression is for me. Not a deep, black hole. Neither a vast ocean of pain, nor a season of storms. My depression is not a long-drawn single day, nor a year of wild, untameable nights. My depression is so all-encompassing as to render all these images null and void. My depression is so run of the mill, so ordinary, it fades into the background like an old, quiet dog.

My depression steals all the light and colour away but then does not know what to do with these things, so, like a not-yet teenage thief, it hides them behind the bins in an unnamed supermarket. My depression is not poetic in any way.

It was the 7th of January 2018 – almost three years ago, but it feels like many lifetimes ago – because it is, of course, it is. M and I had been together just two years but we had, it felt, been through so much that it felt like two decades. Not once, in that entire time, had we spoken of babies. No, that is untrue. Of course we had spoken about babies, one in particular that we loved so dearly. We simply had never spoken of babies that might be *our* babies. Mine and his, whatever way that might look. All around me, babies were being born. All around me, my life felt like it was not my own, like there were no decisions to be made, as though I had no part to play in the way that it would all pan out. I felt lost, sad, confused and alone. I felt an ache in me I had no language to speak of.

On our kitchen table that day there was: a bunch of purple anemones, bought reduced to a pound in Marks & Spencer's, a tree up too long, tall grey candles trying to cut through the grey of my foggy, anxiety-ridden head. I was, that winter, experiencing perhaps the worst period with my mental health in adulthood. I had stopped trying to take my own life but I had, too, stopped trying to live. Each of these feels as dangerous to me, even now, as the other.

I don't want to cry any more. I promised the growing life inside me that I would get better. I would do better. I would *be* better. Yet once again – here I am – with my bullshit.

Locking myself in the bathroom, insisting on taking the dog out alone, hanging around too long in a hospital that's far from safe to be in, trying to keep my sorry-as-fuck-looking face away from people's tired eyes.
Why is it that I am crying though?
A cocktail of too many things to even start to list.
(I try to remember *hope*.)

What right have I got to talk about hope when I can't even find a way to get through a single day without bawling? Is there a way to write about being alive right now that doesn't read like melodrama, or is it just me? Is there a way out of this mess?

I oscillate between sickening, overwhelming brightness and a horrible, fearful melancholy that sits in my gut like a heavy stone. I spent over a month trying to reshape those last two words; to sculpt something less obvious, less basic. It still seemed important to put the words down and to *give* them. Not to anyone in particular, just to take them out and let them find their own place to lay, their own resting ground. What do we mean when we talk about giving, anyway? In this the month where it feels as though it holds such meaning, I can't stop thinking how much this word, this concept, feels to have changed this year. (I wanted to say *shapeshifted* but I'm wary, so wary, of these things I seem to fall back into too easily.) Why am I so obsessed with mythical beings and the changing of their shape? Am I craving a form other than my own? Aren't we all?

Now then.
Back to hope.
Back to giving.
Back to light in dark places.

What does it mean to give?
What does it mean to tend a fire in the cold?
To mind a light in the dark?

'Tonight, the moon holds back / the dark'

I murmur this line over and over. I cannot loosen myself from its soft, insistent hold, its sharp, defiant truth. I think about what it might feel like to allow something to hold back the dark.

This story of the hen and her lost babies has left me moved; overwhelmed.

I already have been thinking, so much this year, about our individual tales of loss, and of our ever newly formed, and still forming, ideas of hope. Sometimes we like to view tales such as this one – a hen who loses her babies through her own song – as being representative of something much bigger, deeper.

What does it mean to hope in such times?

The folklore of this and of so many other lands is full of deep nuance when it comes to such words. Mourning traditions, the sea, boat-building, the healing power of the ash tree – what, if anything, does this mean when we think of, say, climate action?

What might it mean to focus on the sowing of seeds of hope in the face of such individual and collective despair?

How might we clear space, in the middle of such harrowing loss, to start anew – from our centre?

Despair keeps us harboured. I feel as if we are being called to the open sea.

To action that will carry us far from what we deem as safe, and perhaps it is time to listen to that call.

(I try to remember *hope*.)

1st

Now, go out to the night sky, and LOOK UP . . .
(The best poet alive reminding me to keep company with the
moon, ever and always.)

The wreath is hung.
Grew, from seed, every part of it myself, in my first garden.
Last night, just as this first day of the last month of this year
was born, I stood at the front door, looking up at the moon,
with Alice Oswald in my ear. A bright, silent moon above me,
a bright, silent light within me. Never before have I felt so
deeply the power of words, their ability to strengthen and
nourish, their ability to heal us.

Anomaly scan this afternoon, on my own, of course – with M
alone and just as worried – in the car park. There is, inside
me, somehow, a perfectly healthy baby growing. Arrived back
to the cottage to find an (Orkney?) shawl for that healthy,
growing baby, all the way from A on Mull, so beautiful as to
make M and I weep. I could smell her from the wool and the
way it made me feel left me shocked, left me tender. We found
a long hair inside the blue tissue paper, hers, and I held it up
to the light, a stolen auburn offering. When will I see her
again? When will she hold us – all three of us – so close that
her smell is on our skin? In the package, too, a hand-felted
oak leaf, a reminder of so much more than her words could
ever say. And soft white socks – so small and delicate that
suddenly I cannot imagine how I will ever hold this baby in
my arms and not destroy it. How I will ever find a way to
keep it safe. How I will find, somewhere inside me, the guide
to provide safe harbour.

(Never have I seen such tiny socks, felt such excitement arrive
without warning.)

2nd
Shops open again.
20 cents silver glittery deer delivered unimaginable pleasure!

3rd
R sent a copy of her *No Guilt Pregnancy Plan* and of course I cried. Women supporting women, mothers guiding mothers through. It is all too much. And *Expecting* from A, too. I feel so lucky, so looked after, so grateful. Then, long after the post, a large red delivery van brought a tiny grey bonnet – from Z, just like the ones her two wore. Goodness me, my wee emotional head today. Friends, though. What a joy in this life, especially with the year that's in it.
Leaning into the sadness the season brings (without fail) and being gentle with myself. M bought me the Aidan Moffat and RM Hubbert Christmas album – so class for the aul' melancholy of it all, etc. Reminder – just give in to it, get it out of the way quickly.

4th
Good morning winter.
Good morning stars.

The curtains are open, a single candle is lit, and white light dances against the fierce blue ink of the sky.
Siocán, frost, lies outside the window. The doors, now, are open to all that yet might come.

Sat at my desk looking out at the bones of the night, about to wrap a few wee things.
Leftover Celebration Pie for stormy lunch.
Clementines with their leaves still on; the real meaning of Christmas.

5th

I no longer own a single thing that I owned as a child.

I have nothing to pass on to the creature now more than halfway grown inside me.

No photographs, blanket, locks of hair, books or toys. For a variety of reasons outwith my control I am not able to seek these things back, even those that still exist, and I have had to find ways to make peace with their unmarked loss. What can I pass from my own self on to this newly forming gift of blood and bone?

My lover used to roll his eyes when I came home from the fields with porcelain-white bones, the bog with hauntingly delicate cotton flowers, the laneways with lichen-covered sticks, the shore with seed-heads carried over vast, tumultuous seas.
Now, as time has passed — as it is wont to do — he has begun to bring such delicacies, too, into our home; offered into my grateful, open hands. He knows, now — I think he does — that these found objects are things that I must keep close to me, near enough to see & hold & stroke. In the place of so much else that has been lost.

Suddenly, without any warning, I find myself thinking, once more, about that dead goldfinch.
I am filled with thoughts of rites & traditions, of respect & creaturely rot.
I think of the beetroot leaves and poppy heads with which I covered its body:
the red of it all, the hushed ceremony.

How the yellow of its broken wing
glimmered
in the early light of morning.

How the black of its wee mangled body
beside the flame-red made me think of a
cinnabar moth, from a different season,
a different place, a different world.

How the whole day carried a trace of its
stopped heart: fragile grace, suspended in ashen, hallowed air.

Made the mistake of reading that *Examiner* piece that was all
over Instagram about labouring alone and wish I hadn't
bothered.
Fuck it all, every last bit of it, why is it always women left
carrying the load? This government would sicken you.

6th
Goodnight.
(REMEMBER LIGHT.)
Hospital. My work trousers don't fit any more, which brings
me incomparable joy.
Reviewed Sophie Mackintosh's incredible *Blue Ticket*. So many
exceptionally moving lines, but this one – the protagonist's
explanation for wanting to have a baby, a dream of her daughter
– I found particularly so: 'She moves in the way of ancient and
eternal things.'
Oh my goodness, these words.

Second light of Advent, light of plants.
(I have so many poppy heads I am at a loss as to where there
is left to put them.)

7th

In the post, thought lost but finally here, the baby's first doll, bought from a Steiner Mamma. Not to be given for quite some time but this felt important for me to do although I am unsure why.

Manchán's new book arrived from Red Fox Press, and it is the stuff of dreams.
Read, in one sitting, after M made us a delightful veggie brunch.
Instagram sending me updates about this day last year, when J and I drank Nosecco and took pictures of our nails and suddenly I am back there, in Dublin, after a full day of mooching, with someone I love, and I am so lonely – insufferably so. Got the most beautiful vintage baubles out to console myself because yes, I am that shallow. White chocolate and *The Snow Goose* in bed. A dream end to a weird day.

8th

First vaccine on the island of Ireland happening North this morning.
The frosty fog has lifted for the first time in days and the darkness that's been revealed is lit by winter stars, steeped in near silence. Three candles lit in our home: for those lost, for those suffering, for hope.
Genevieve Dutton's words on the comfort in the darkness were oh so soothing today, pure gorgeousness.

How the hydrangea catch the light and seem as if they reflect it back, even in their skeletal, near-gone state. I want to say more but I will have to come back to it. Oh my goodness this tiredness though.

9th
Just one day after reading her beautiful words, received, in the post, the most exquisite woven hanging and hand-dipped beeswax candle from G. Light moulded in the darkness. Women are the answer, always.

Woke, in the grey afternoon, from a dream in which I took the bábóg inside me to Cornwall. I swam, with a much rounder belly than now, in turquoise waters, rippling so gently.
(How will I ever go back to being a body that doesn't have another body dancing inside it?)

M put the most ridiculous vintage Santa lights up in our wee kitchen, then fed the tired old dog chorizo in bed – and I think both these have made me love him twice as much as before.

10th
Photo shoot for the *Independent*. 5 a.m. start at 22 weeks pregnant but oh my god to see Dublin again after so long, to be with other people, to see the Christmas lights on my own. I am over the bleeding moon.

11th
the moon the moon
the moonmoonmoon

Received a gift of Emily Dickinson's envelope poems from E which made me glad indeed.

12th
Woke up this morning to my lover playing The Waitresses'
Christmas song up full pelt whilst making coffee and mince
pies. 2020 is not going out with a bang, rather with making
the most of every single moment and being so bleeding grateful
for every single thing we have.

13th
Painted my nails pistachio.
Wee one dancing along inside me to Mister Edwyn Collins.

14th

   I thought it was wind

. . . that had taken to playing my insides like an ancient
instrument.
An instrument of fine bone: creaturely and slender,
like that swan in the documentary I wasn't able to watch.
Wild and howling at times, rattling at my ribs like the Cailleach;
goddess of the hearth, inside my cage.

Then, at other moments – so gentle as to feel more like a
flickering – like a perfectly formed glow-worm; grown wings.

   I thought it must be coming from outside;

that shimmering, spiralling feeling inside my belly.
That it must be the weather, just.
Only the weather.
That it must be only the wind finding places to hide.

(Will never get over the fact another body moved inside of
mine.)

15th

Hydrangea, against the once-white walls, like rust on gorgeous, abandoned objects.

The winter's beautiful bones, in the shelter of the speckled thrush.

G says, on her Instagram: 'Things will be better by the time the swifts come back,' and I cry. That's how things go these days.

From K, in the post, an egg painted with inks she herself has made. I am so so lucky, the baby is too.

16th

Early train again to Dublin in the storm for pictures in the storm.

Joy.

17th

M made me the most perfect candleholder for Advent.

Candles lit for the whole day, which helps such an awful lot indeed.

Light of beasts, as the dog snores at my feet.

18th

Have found myself, in the depths of the darkest half of the year, on the cusp of the turning, thinking of swallows. How they swooped and wheeled in the sky, above a garden full of wren-song. Remembering the pelvic girdle of a delicately bird-like rat, given by my lover. Found as he cleared away shoots springing up beside the dead ash tree. Thinking about April's seed-pink moon, as the world ached and broke, and made room for healing.

Of how different next April might be.

23 weeks today.

19th
Baby's first swim in Dublin.
Thrilling.

Reminder: you are enough.
Everything is going to be OK.

20th
Hazy, frosty sunrise in the fields this morning was nothing
short of divine. Birds singing their hearts out. Beams and lines
of bright gold. Tomorrow the sun will dance, just so, at
Newgrange – at all the places our ancestors built – in honour
of the returning light. Very few of us will see it anywhere aside
from our own homes; the places closest to us. The womb of
mother earth will hold space for the return of the light; just
when my own is full.

Wee one inside of me, carrying back the light.

I close my eyes, allow myself to imagine, for the very first time
properly, their small face.
I see it bathed in morning light.
A path of it from the sky to the soft circle of their cheek.
A path of light.

I always thought this was the longest night.

Sky all the blues that ever existed.
Moon – a startlingly beautiful crescent.
So much sorrow as everything changes yet again for folk.
Loneliness, and too much to even contemplate.

Last light before solstice.

Blush-pink rose beside lady's mantle still in bloom.
Watched Saturn & Jupiter hold each other, close as lovers.

A Christmas star, the first for centuries,
above our first garden.

Wee drummer inside me, playing on my belly,
as I pull out both the leeks.

I wish I'd known, long before now,
that sowing is an act of trust.

That the body, as it sows & plants, when it tends land,
as it hopes for growth,
gives itself over to a vast & shifting future
it could never, in that moment, quite imagine.

I wish I'd known that to sow
is to scatter light around,
like wee fluttering moths.

They are coming,

they are coming,

It is winter.

Epilogue

First Sunday of Advent, 2021
Lizard Peninsula, Cornwall

It was so dark, that first winter we spent there.

There was more darkness to the nights' skies than
ever either of us had known before.
The kind of darkness that takes the light that's hung around
the place and makes it brighter, brighter, much more bright,
by far . . .

. . . And what of those moths?

EPILOGUE

Those moths that came & came & came; refusing to leave?

I began, slowly, to write of them.
I drew their forms with pencil marks at dawn . . .

Looking back, two years in, I see how much it all meant to me, the presence of those winged creatures in my life. It all happened in the way that things are sometimes wont to in the winter – cautiously, fearfully, silently – with restless, shivery hands. I need you to know that, just before the world changed for ever, they came.

That it was winter.

I need for you to know that somehow, in the depths of winter, they came.

At the beginning I begged with them to leave.

Look at this place, I wailed, at their velvety, insect bodies. *Look at all this work there is yet to do.*

Pleading would not cut it, though. They took to sleeping on my body then at night, sweet, ancient breath on skin – the beat of them – in my hair, in my dreams, in my bones. I put out every light, blocked up all the hollow places. Still, even then, I would find them sleeping in the nests of every bird. Amidst stinging nettles, in the drainpipe, on the thyme, across the flight-path of the hunting wren – on the radio, in my dreams, in those that others' had of me – I could not find a place in which to hide. They came through windows, down the chimney, across boundaries, over barriers. The moths came, the moths came. The moths came and that is really all there is to tell. I took them out, gave them back to the crow-black night — but they waited for me, still, at the door.

They came and there was nothing I could do, no action I could take, no words that I could mutter, that would keep the moths from coming if I tried.
   I listed them, I named them, I hallowed them. I finally let them settle beneath my skin . . .

That long-drawn winter is long gone, of course, but it left its moths & birds, its nests & bones, in its wake.

Slowly, with the passing nights, I have begun to understand it all.

That year that came along and changed our lives.

                                        . . . *it is (still) winter.*

All this time spent telling you of one stone cottage.

A small dwelling on an isolated laneway in the middle of an equally small island.
A westerly part of Europe; right where the land gives itself over to the sea.
The only place in the world I have ever sown seeds into the soil.
The only time in my life I have watched them bloom & unfurl, collected their seeds for the new year – as the life inside them turned itself outside in.

I have told you about a wild, quiet stretch of land.
Never have I known anywhere as closely as I have known that garden; known somewhere so intimately as there.
Never have I known a dwelling place so well as to know it in winter, stripped & skeletal, so seductively & suddenly bare.
It almost breaks me into wee small pieces, shards of glass, to think of leaving here properly, even though I know it's best for our family.

It's not about the house, or the laneway, or the county, or the island.

I feel broken, I realise, by the thought of leaving the place we made the seed that grew into our son. The piece of ground on which we stood with white plastic in our hands, a white moon in the sky, and a blue line singing out to us like fox cubs.

He came, you see.
    That long-drawn year passed, as always they do.
    After the solstice, Christmas, a freshly born year, a baby.
    He came in the spring, of course.

We stayed there, in that place, my lover, the dog, me and him.
We stayed until December arrived, once more, still and white
and full of stars.
That place where, just the day before he came, I sowed seeds
into the earth.
The place I stood with him in my arms, howling with confusion & with love, with fear & with hope – as meteors flashed
across the postpartum belly of the sky.
The place where I finally let go of all the guilt & the shame
& the anxiety.
This garden where I felt parts 'of me soften, pink & quiet.
The place where I realised nothing would ever be the same again
(and that that was both harrowing and gorgeous all in one).

This garden where I became the only thing that I will always
be.

I've long been drawn to Wabi–Sabi – a world view based on
the acceptance of transience and imperfection that speaks to
the Buddhist ideal of existence: nothing lasts, nothing is finished,
nothing is perfect.

Time and time again, since my son was born, I've felt that if
anything could summarise the vast changes in me since
becoming a mother – perhaps it is this.

No given moment will stay for ever.
No feeling will remain always.
New days, when they come, carry the hope that things will
be brighter, lighter.

When I think about the idea of things being carried, these days, I cannot help but think of my son. Not just because of these obvious facts: I carried him, inside of my body, until it was safe for his body to come out to meet the body of the earth. I have carried him, almost all day, every single day since he was born. In my arms, wrapped around my chest, strapped to my back, asleep, awake (and all of the stages in between), facing out to the world; facing into the body in which he grew, in Ireland, in England, on a boat that carried the pair of us across the sea to Wales. I carry a small pebble on my person every single day of life, a star marked onto its surface, given to me in the early days he was inside me by a dear stone-carving friend. I carry the weight of every single thing in the world – on my shoulders, in my stomach, on my mind, etched onto my pelt – since less than an hour after he was born. He carried, in those early, milky, foggy days, so little weight on his wee bird-body that all I ever thought of was weight.
The weight of things I had never even once considered before.

My wee one was born with tongue tie,
meaning he could not, at first,
feed himself from my body.

My wee one was born with the full pink moon,
meaning he carried the weight of the night sky
in his newly formed, slender hands.

He was named for the moon & for poetry & for a wild river.
Impermanent things, unfinished things, imperfect things.

You see *he carried them with him*, his names, our son did.

He was named for the red that followed him around, that shapeshifted each morning of that first week. Red that faded into pink right before my eyes.

Hues that I couldn't quite get out of my head: colour-worm. My son was named for a moon that refused to stand still long enough for me to photograph it, neither before or after I breathed him out of my insides, like a song.

Since he arrived, I've spent every journey we've made in the back seat of the car we bought when we knew he really was coming along. I've spent so much time in that space, one I had never even been in before he came, that I recently dreamed I lived there.

Going through the 'Notes' section on my phone one morning with the weight of his body on mine, I found a secret.

BIRD OF LIGHT in the back seat of the car.

That day I had wept like a baby. It was an experience the like of which you hear about but assume will never happen to you, beautiful, haunting. And I would have forgotten it for ever, this experience, in a dim haze, perhaps, without this note . . .

Back when the summer sun had been making its way away, far from us, my lover dragged us out of bed to take us to the sea. I needed it more than I can put into words, really, and on the way home the sun played with my phone, making a shimmery, exquisite dance on the roof of the car. Our son made a sound he had never made before; a laugh the like of which I had never heard – over and over – looking at me like I'd placed the whole world into his small hands. My wee bird, laughing at a bird of light, in the back seat of our car. I'm not sure what it was that made me so emotional when I recounted it in my diary that night, exhaustion, mawkishness, overwhelm, joy? An emotion I don't have a name for, still so embedded in the mud of matrescence, but that many others recognise, too? A handshake, a cult film, a lullaby in the language of a lost home?

Going through pictures on that same phone later I discover that the only one out of 8,679 that has 'Home' as its auto location is one of me in the same back seat. The only part of my body in the shot is my lap. A set of random objects are the true stars of the show: a nursing shawl given by a dear friend when we struggled to feed, the bag I carry my son's things in, his favourite pom-pom hat, his first bear – given to him by one of the most beautiful women I know despite only having met her once – and the reusable cup I bought with my closest friend at the last Port Eliot Festival, one of the last things I did alone before the world changed for ever.

I want to tell you more about this image, to say more about these objects; the sheer fucking poetry of it all – but I am so tired. I am so caught up in the living of it, I suppose.

When I started this book I had, only just that week, begun the process of moving from the small stone house of which I have been trying to tell you. Alongside the Word document that grew into this book, there were browsers open on my laptop with beautiful old tenement flats for rent in Glasgow in an attempt to move there with my family. Only a handful of weeks passed before the location had changed; we were considering Cornwall then, just as we considered Bristol before Glasgow. Several months passed with the idea in mind that we might just use the wee bit of money we'd managed to put away to buy a van and take to the road. Or a boat, any old vessel that could manage any old stretch of water, in fact.

This, for me, has been the biggest learning of my life; the hardest, greatest gift.

The sense that HOME might not actually be about *place* at all.

I feel at home stood at the sick sycamore at the foot of the garden of this cottage of which I have told you.

I feel at home looking at Cornish coves on Instagram that I've never seen in real life.

I feel at home when I pass the hospital where our son was born despite having no other connection to that grey Irish midland town whatsoever.

I feel at home in myself, despite how hard new motherhood is, how changed I feel, how unknown my own bones.

If I'm honest, the place I might feel most at home is in fact the back seat of a car I can't even drive.

Holding my son's hand until he falls asleep.

My lover singing along in funny voices to songs on the radio.

The three of us together; no matter where we are headed.

Perhaps *mother* is just
another word for *home*.
Perhaps home is just
another word for *safe*,
or *content*,
or *whole* . . .

I feel safe; I feel content; I feel whole.

I feel at home.
I am your home.
I am home.

Acknowledgements

I AM GRATEFUL TO MY AGENT Kirsty McLachlan, who is always such a quiet, defining feature in the landscape of everything I write.

At Canongate I am grateful to everyone who played a part in the making of this book: Simon Thorogood, Leila Cruickshank, Vicki Rutherford, Rebecca Bonallie, Jamie Norman, Claire Reiderman, Rali Chorbadzhiyska, Lucy Zhou and Rafaela Romaya. Many thanks to Vasilisa Romanenko for the beautiful cover illustration.

Deepest thanks to Sharon McTeir who sat with me over and over working with white space as though we were dancing in a soft, pink dawn.

To all the supportive early readers of the book, I am ever grateful.

To Manchán Magan for guidance with the Irish language, and for his friendship, always.

To all in my life who lend their light, I am heart-glad to know you.

I am a grateful recipient of a Literature Bursary from the Arts Council of Ireland, which greatly supported me during the writing of this book. I wrote this under the shelter of the home of Zoe Hawes and am grateful beyond measure for her presence at that time.

Early sections have appeared in the following publications: *In the Garden* (Daunt Books, Spring '21), *The New Frontier: Contemporary Writing from & About the Irish Border* (New Island Books, Autumn '21), *Impermanence* (No Alibis Press, Summer '22), *Winter Papers 6*, *Dark Mountain* Issue 19 and *Extra Teeth* Issue Four – and online at the National Centre for Writing. I am grateful for the stellar work of the editors of these in making this work much better than how it began.

I am grateful beyond measure to my lover, our son and our dog, who are my safe place; my morning song; my winter light on snow, falling.

This was written during a time of great change in my life; about a time during which everything, as well as nothing at all, seemed to change with each passing day. I wrote under the darkening cover of postnatal depression, at a time when I was unsure light would ever find a way back. And I suppose it feels a little silly – preposterous? – to say this but it would be improper not to: most of all I am grateful to this book. To these pages; these words; this reminder of what it means to be alive.

It is not lost on me that during the darkest days I have known, my job was to sit and write about light.

In the longest, loneliest winter of my life, the only expectation placed on me – outwith mothering – was to write about nests, and swallows, and newly born hope.

There is much to be grateful for, indeed.

Permission Credits

Manus Kenny

KERRI NÍ DOCHARTAIGH's first book, *Thin Places*, was published in Spring 2022 in the US. It was an Indies Introduce selection for Winter/Spring 2022, an Indie Next selection for April 2022, and A Junior Library Guild selection for Spring 2022.

Cacophony of Bone is her second book. She lives in the west of Ireland with her family.

milkweed
EDITIONS

Founded as a nonprofit organization in 1980, Milkweed Editions is an independent publisher. Our mission is to identify, nurture, and publish transformative literature, and build an engaged community around it.

Milkweed Editions is based in Bdé Óta Othúŋwe (Minneapolis) within Mní Sota Makhóčhe, the traditional homeland of the Dakhóta people. Residing here since time immemorial, Dakhóta people still call Mní Sota Makhóčhe home, with four federally recognized Dakhóta nations and many more Dakhóta people residing in what is now the state of Minnesota. Due to continued legacies of colonization, genocide, and forced removal, generations of Dakhóta people remain disenfranchised from their traditional homeland. Presently, Mní Sota Makhóčhe has become a refuge and home for many Indigenous nations and peoples, including seven federally recognized Ojibwe nations. We humbly encourage our readers to reflect upon the historical legacies held in the lands they occupy.

milkweed.org

Milkweed Editions, an independent nonprofit publisher, gratefully acknowledges sustaining support from our Board of Directors; the Alan B. Slifka Foundation and its president, Riva Ariella Ritvo-Slifka; the Amazon Literary Partnership; the Ballard Spahr Foundation; *Copper Nickel*; the McKnight Foundation; the National Endowment for the Arts; the National Poetry Series; and other generous contributions from foundations, corporations, and individuals. Also, this activity is made possible by the voters of Minnesota through a Minnesota State Arts Board Operating Support grant, thanks to a legislative appropriation from the arts and cultural heritage fund. For a full listing of Milkweed Editions supporters, please visit milkweed.org.

Typeset in Bembo

Bembo was created in the 1920s under the direction
of printing historian Stanley Morison for the Monotype
Corporation. Bembo is based upon the 1495 design cut by
Francesco Griffo for Aldus Manutius, and named after the first
book to use the typeface, a small book called *De Aetna*, by the
Italian poet and cleric Pietro Bembo.